from the classroom
to the corner

Studies in the
Postmodern Theory of Education

Joe L. Kincheloe and Shirley R. Steinberg
General Editors

Vol. 302

PETER LANG
New York • Washington, D.C./Baltimore • Bern
Frankfurt am Main • Berlin • Brussels • Vienna • Oxford

Cynthia Cole Robinson

from the classroom
to the corner

Female Dropouts' Reflections
on Their School Years

To Vera
I remember Sturling
at NLU together and
it great to Be working with
you in the Same department!
Cynthia 2.27.07

PETER LANG
New York • Washington, D.C./Baltimore • Bern
Frankfurt am Main • Berlin • Brussels • Vienna • Oxford

Library of Congress Cataloging-in-Publication Data

Robinson, Cynthia Cole.
From the classroom to the corner: female dropouts' reflections
on their school years / Cynthia Cole Robinson.
p. cm. — (Counterpoints; v. 302)
Includes bibliographical references.
1. High school dropouts—Illinois—Chicago—Case studies. 2. Women—
Education—Illinois—Chicago—Case studies. 3. Child prostitutes—Illinois—
Chicago—Case studies. 4. Educational sociology—Illinois—Chicago—
Case studies. I. Title. II. Series: Counterpoints (New York, N.Y.); v. 302.
LC146.7.I3R63   373.12'9130977311—dc22   2006012709
ISBN-13: 978-0-8204-8189-0
ISBN-10: 0-8204-8189-0
ISSN 1058-1634

Bibliographic information published by **Die Deutsche Bibliothek**.
Die Deutsche Bibliothek lists this publication in the "Deutsche
Nationalbibliografie"; detailed bibliographic data is available
on the Internet at http://dnb.ddb.de/.

Cover design by Lisa Barfield

The paper in this book meets the guidelines for permanence and durability
of the Committee on Production Guidelines for Book Longevity
of the Council of Library Resources.

© 2007 Peter Lang Publishing, Inc., New York
29 Broadway, 18th floor, New York, NY 10006
www.peterlang.com

Printed in the United States of America

For my brothers, James and Stephen Cole

For my daughter, Payton Olivia Robinson

For my husband, Michael Dion Robinson

Most of all,

For the
Young
Women
Who
Shared
Their
Souls
With Me,
I was honored by your presence; I hope I have served you well.

Table of Contents

Preface ix

Acknowledgments xxiii

Forgotten: A Poem xxvii

Part One: Setting the Backdrop

Chapter One
Female Dropouts and Prostitution 3

Chapter Two
Feminist Theory and Prostitution 21

Chapter Three
Curriculum Theory and Dropping Out: The Nonschool Curriculum 37

Part Two: In Their Own Words

Chapter Four
"Nobody Cares": A Perspective from the Front Line 49
by Stephen Cole

Chapter Five
Carmella's Story: "My Baby Didn't Have
No Pampers and No Milk" 57

Chapter Six:
Celina's Story: "I Can't See Myself Standing on No Corner" 109

Chapter Seven
Voyage to Buddha: "I Needed Some Place to Stay" 143

Part Three: Getting an Understanding

Chapter Eight
Getting an Understanding 173

Chapter Nine
Conclusions 185

Notes 195

References 197

Preface

"Where's Elisha?" This question was beginning to be a part of my morning routine as I took the roll in my class. The replies from her classmates were always the same, as students in her homeroom called out that she was not present for the attendance roll call; she was absent yet again. I talked with one of her girlfriends to ask her why Elisha was absent so frequently; she described her home situation as one in which she was the eldest sibling of five in a household headed by her mother, a single parent. They had financial difficulties and Elisha had taken a job at the local grocery store to help make ends meet. Maybe that would explain why she was slouched over and incoherent many times when she attended school. However, I was concerned about her since she was one of my sharpest students, never hesitating to share her well thought out ideas or lead class discussions. In spite of the fact that she was truant, she was able to quickly pick up on classroom assignments and discussions when she was present. Buried under a sea of papers, I promised myself that I would call her mother over the weekend, but never had the chance.

That same weekend, I happened to be out very early, driving on a main street when I noticed a woman standing on the corner scantily clad, perusing the passing cars as she smiled and waved. I took special notice because this was an area I was familiar with and had never seen solicitation by prostitutes there. As I sat at the stoplight, I was able to get a good look at the woman. It turned out the woman was a girl. It was Elisha. There she stood, brazen and totally out of the character I had come to know. That entire weekend I was confused and upset. What would I say to her if she came to school on Monday morning? Should I share this with any of the faculty members or administrators at school? Should I call her mother? When Monday morning arrived, I shared the incident with a veteran teacher, since she had been at the school for 25 years; I figured she would know what we could do to handle it.

She didn't. We dropped the ball, and Elisha dropped us; she never returned to school.

That was years ago. I have often worried about Elisha and my failure to respond in a more helpful manner, my failure and the school's failure to address the needs and issues of such girls. It was not until that next fall that I realized that many more young girls are in her same predicament. This issue of school-age girls prostituting could not go unaddressed as I spent an evening on a police beat with my brother, a police officer (author of Chapter 4, "Nobody Cares") in a red light district. During the 12 hours of that patrol, we talked to about 25 prostitutes, at least 20 of whom were under the age of 18. I could not help but think about Elisha and the fact that these girls should have been in bed that night resting for the next school day. Many of them float in and out of classrooms, unnoticed and unaddressed. They should have been my students. Instead, they had moved from the classroom to the corner. I asked myself, "How does this happen? How do they view promises of traditional schooling, i.e., career and life opportunities? How do they view school and what was their schooling experience like? What is lacking in schools when prostitution seems to be the only answer for these girls? What prompted them to drop out and lead this alternative life?"

These are some of the questions to which I yearned to know the answer, so I went on a scavenger hunt of sorts to find literature explaining girls like Elisha. In my search, I found that there have been numerous studies on the lives of males who withdraw from the school system or "drop out" (Dowdwell, 1996; Mungo, 1992); however, the amount of literature and research on girls who drop out pales in comparison. Many boys living alternative lifestyles steeped in criminal activities such as theft, gang-related activity, and drug dealing are dropouts and often base their transition into these lifestyles on the fact that they have little traditional earning power (Baron, 2001; Wilson, 1997; Padilla, 1992; Anderson, 1990; Sullivan, 1989; Williams, 1989; MacLeod, 1987).[1] While the drop-out rate among girls is approximately the same as that of boys (Kaufman, et al., 2000; EDC, 1990; Earle & Roach, 1989), there are fewer in-depth analyses of the alternatives that females turn to when they do not follow traditional life tracks (i.e., schooling, careers, etc.).

When I first began to research female dropouts who find themselves working as adolescent prostitutes due to a lack of education or job training, I had no idea that this research would lead me to the topic of my dissertation. In fact, I was taking a qualitative research class in which I had to write a mock dissertation proposal. Since part of the project was a review of literature, I figured that I could find more answers to why I'd found so many girls on the street that night instead of in bed, sound asleep, resting for the upcoming school day. I had the idea that I could really research something that meant something to me and could bring some clarity to what often haunted my brother, at the end of his patrol on Harry Hines Boulevard, a red-light district. Before then, dissertation research to me seemed to be a form of academic hazing.

As I began the process, I was surprised to find that little literature existed on female adolescent prostitution, and virtually none existed about the in-school experiences of such girls. Because I was really driven to understand this, I continued to research and instead ended up with a literature review that pieced together literature on female dropouts, adolescent prostitution, Black feminism, and Alice Walker's womanism.

Every time I told people what my research topic was, I could see in their faces that they were perplexed. In fact, some academics even asked if I had any experience in it myself. You see, one usually gets associated with what he or she researches; if you research queer theory, you must be gay. If you research African American teachers or students, some would argue that you should be African American. The standpoint theorists would be disappointed to learn that, in fact, I never was a dropout or a prostitute though I've always been a female. In fact, one such standpoint theorist was in an advanced qualitative research class in which she berated me for having the audacity to research prostitution since I had never been a prostitute. In the class we often shared our writing, and this particular evening I was reading a part of my review of literature about the fact that many Black prostitutes often state that they are treated much worse than their White counterparts, and that they are paid less and are oftentimes requested to act in stereotypically "ghetto" roles by their clients. My colleague, who was both a former prostitute and White, was infuriated by this. She said that prostitution was like a sisterhood in which racial boundaries didn't exist. I replied by saying that racial boundaries exist in every facet of life and that I wasn't sharing my own point of view; that, in fact, I was reviewing literature from Guidorz (1996). To which she responded, "I don't know if I should throw up, run from the room, or slap the shit out of you." My professor at the time, Bill Ayers, quickly addressed her comment, things settled down, and we were able to continue on with class. Ironically, she and I became friends after that. These types of standpoint theory exchanges often occurred in that class; my friend Greg Michie was often confronted about his research which grew into *Holler if You Hear Me*, and his doctoral research (which became *See You When We Get There*). Some of our Latino classmates took issue with him as a White man writing about the Latino community and the school in which he taught. In that class I cemented the idea that I identified as a womanist, since I tended to look at things from a more inclusive perspective. I came to the conclusion that I was more concerned with the stories being shared than who was sharing them. Also, I decided that I would use Black feminism as a theoretical framework, and case studies by way of oral history tended to lend voice to these young women who were marginalized and voiceless. So I tried to remove as much as possible from their oral histories, though I am there as an editor and a narrator. In my editing, I left out a great deal of what the young women had shared with me, as they told me things that they had never shared with anyone before and I felt that it would violate the bond we had formed.

Another perspective that I encountered during the course of my research was that of "putting business in the street" or "airing dirty laundry," as we call it in the African American community. When I was younger, I thought that this was only a cultural taboo for the African American community, but later learned that it is quite a cross-cultural concept. Once, during a book discussion with other teacher educators about misperceptions of the African American community and the incorrect assumption that African American parents in the inner city don't care about their children's education, I shared that African American parents care a great deal about their children's academic success and view it as the only way to a better life. I shared that many people don't consider the fact that the parents are working jobs where taking off work to go to the school could mean the loss of their job. Many are dealing with socioeconomic issues that middle-class people don't know anything about. I began to share some of my stories describing how I grew up in a working-class, poor neighborhood on the south side of Chicago, and knew a great deal about these issues. Later, one of my African American colleagues scolded me indirectly, saying, "It's not my job to educate White folks on the secrets of the Black community." I didn't reply because I was so taken aback and thought the exact opposite; I think it is exactly my business to educate teacher educators on the African American community, since they are sending other teachers into our community who will do much more harm than good without an understanding of the community in which they teach and the people who live in it.

Secrets can be a dangerous thing. I'm very leery of secrets kept by families or communities, as these secrets are usually a cesspool of atrocities that will continue to fester at the expense of some unsuspecting soul. For instance, take child molestation. The keeping of such a secret usually leads to another victim, who must struggle to become a survivor.

I've often struggled with research that focuses on how some problem happened, as it is viewed by many as a deficit model or blaming the victim. But it is true that if we don't understand why or how, we will never be able to assist in addressing a thing. In my research, I address the in-school and out-of-school experiences of female dropouts who find themselves in adolescent prostitution; however, I also address what worked in the school environment and what did not work from their perspective and in their own words.

Intention of Research

This research is aimed at addressing that gap in the literature on dropouts by studying the lived experiences of girls who leave traditional schooling and turn to prostitution, and are thus educated by their interactions with their living environments, peers, or through daily activities or what is known as the nonschool curriculum. Nonschool forms of education are also known as the out-of-school curriculum, referring to what students learn from their home environment, community, and peers (Schubert, 1986). The study of adolescent female prostitutes is important since approximately 80% or more of adolescent prostitutes are dropouts (Weisberg, 1985; Fisher et al., 1982; James, 1980; Silbert et al., 1980; Enablers, 1978; Gray, 1973).

Many adolescent females involved in prostitution state that they had negative experiences in school and have or had a very unfavorable opinion of schools. Although they state that their lack of education and thus lack of adequate employment played a role in their turning to prostitution and/or remaining in the industry, they remain pessimistic about education (Johnson, 1992). Thus, the educational experiences (both in and out of school) of these young women are critical to understanding why the school system did not work for them. This research can give insight into how to help schools serve the needs of girls who are on the verge of dropping out.

Thus, the purpose of this research is to examine the educational experiences (both in and out of school) of female adolescent dropouts who support themselves through prostitution. Therefore, the three issues that intersect in this study are (1) female dropouts, (2) the in-school and out-of-school curriculum, and (3) female adolescent prostitution. While research has been conducted on adolescent prostitution, there have not been any studies that focus primarily on the educational experiences of these young women. This education-focused research is important, since previous studies on adolescent prostitution stated that these girls enter and remain in prostitution due to lack of adequate employment and education. Research on the schooling experiences of these girls is needed, as studies have indicated that dropping out of school and prostitution are highly correlated (Johnson, 1992; Weisberg, 1985; Silbert & Pines, 1982; Enablers, 1978; Gray, 1973).[2]

I examined three intersecting phenomena using a womanist theoretical framework, as well as feminist research methodology to explore them. A womanist framework and research methodology is important in this study because all of the phenomena deal with marginalization, as girls are silenced in schools and classrooms (Henry, 1998; Sadker & Sadker, 1994) which leads to the withdrawal from the school system for some. Students, both female and male, are not included in composing curricula that are taught in schools. Furthermore, educational experiences outside of the classroom are not addressed in school; hence, the out-of-school curriculum is marginalized by administrators, teachers, and others. Lastly, adolescent prostitution is marginalized from the feminist conversation in that much of the feminist literature on prostitution deals with adult women, not adolescents. For these reasons, the overarching theoretical framework and research methodology is feminism, while specific feminist/womanist theories were used to discuss the issue of prostitution.

There is a wealth of research on female prostitutes; this study differs in the perspective from which the issue will be examined and in the research methodology. This research focuses on prostitution as an organically adolescent issue, meaning that the majority of females enter the field of prostitution at age 14, or younger. It is also comprehensive in that it focuses on various issues that lead adolescents to prostitution, such as: (1) physical and sexual abuse in their living situations; (2) social isolation, as many do not build social support relationships and networks; and (3) educational failure due to an educational system that they feel does not present opportunities that will work in their lives and does not address their needs, leading them to withdraw or drop out. A feminist epistemology is employed to address issues of empowerment, such as economic and educational opportunities for this very marginalized and silenced group of young women. Ironically, though prostitutes are among the most exploited women, the feminist movement did not include the plight of these women until 15 years ago (Brock, 1998); thus, the feminist movement has marginalized prostitutes in that it has not addressed issues unique to their situation. The feminist perspective that most closely addresses some of the class and exploitation issues that prostitutes face—though not entirely—is Black feminism, in that it posits that Black women suffer oppression not addressed by mainstream feminism due to a legacy of slavery that exploited Black women as concubines of White slave masters, and examines their place in the political economy (hooks, 1981). Though Black feminism speaks directly to the condition of Black women, a womanist framework is employed, as female adolescent prostitution is an epidemic that crosses the boundaries of race and ethnicity. Lastly, though there is a wealth of research on prostitution, there is a need for research that gives voice to these young women. Voice can be defined as a liberating and political force that allows one to explore his or her own authentic self-identity, unapologetically (hooks, 1989; Romo-Carmona, 1987; Lorde, 1984). The concept of voice I used can be best defined by Romo-Carmona:

> Each time a woman begins to speak, a liberating process begins, one that is unavoidable and has powerful political implications. In these pages we see repeated the process of self-discovery, of affirmation in coming out of the closet, the search for a definition of our identity within the family and our community, the search for answers, for meaning in our personal struggles, and the commitment to a political struggle to end all forms of oppression. The stages of increasing awareness become clear when we begin to recount the story of our lives to someone else, someone who has experienced the same changes. When we write or speak about these changes we establish our experiences as valid and real, we begin to analyze, and that analysis gives us the necessary perspective to place our lives in a context where we know what to do next. (Romo-Carmona, 1987, p. xxi)

The majority of existing research does not include the voices of the prostitutes. My research methodology differs in that feminist case study is used and the research methods include interviews and oral history, which lends itself to the actual voices, experiences, and expressions of these young women. Through this research, it is possible that programs could be created to help girls who are at risk of entering such a lifestyle.

Methodology

Theoretical Framework/Philosophical Orientation

Since one of the goals of feminism is to validate and make known the unique experiences of women, it is appropriate to use this theoretical framework to approach female dropouts who have left traditional schooling. Because feminist theory examines the objectification and commodification of women, it is a great theoretical tool for studying the issue of prostitution. Feminist theory also posits that women's experiences are excluded from what is considered to be valuable knowledge; therefore, it is useful for studying curricular issues such as the nonschool or out-of-school curriculum. According to nonschool curricularists, the personal aspects of student lives are omitted from the classroom (Schubert, 1981; Delpit, 1995; Foster, 1995; Miller, 1993). This issue lends itself to feminist theorizing because it reflects the same issues of marginalization that women have experienced in the past and in the present. So the three issues of adolescent women being studied—dropping out, prostitution, and nonschool curriculum—all can be explored through the lens of feminism.

Feminist Methodology

Qualitative research consists of a myriad of methodologies as it seeks to understand people's perspectives of the world and their own socially constructed realities. As people and their perceptions vary, the method of relaying these realities should reflect this diversity. Feminist research methodology is one strand of qualitative research that lends itself to the diversity of participants as well as to the marginalized groups of people.

Feminist research methodological theory is a perspective or way of seeing women's lived experiences. It can be more accurately described as a myriad of existing methodologies; however, in some instances feminist researchers create original methodologies to suit specific research needs (Reinharz, 1992). The one qualifying characteristic of the borrowed or altered methodologies used in feminist research methodology is that they lend themselves to in-depth examinations of participants, thus allowing their voices to be heard. Some of these methodologies are oral history, phenomenology, case study, action research, interview, and ethnography.

Feminist research methodology is eclectic in the methods it employs in an effort to ensure that it does not speak for or exclude the voices of the participants. I emphasize participants here because it is a misguided assumption that feminist research has to be by or about women as a whole (Ristock & Pennell, 1996).[3] There is great diversity within feminism and among feminists; therefore, feminism and feminist research methodology reflect this diversity, resulting in a variety of divisions of feminism—some based on race, class, and sexual orientation. As stated by feminist researcher Carolyn

Burke (1978), "The strength of the women's movement lies in its ability to acknowledge 'serious disagreement' on topics including feminist methods" (p. 855).

In order to ensure that the voices of these young women are heard, member checks were conducted with the participants reassure that a reliable account of the participant is presented. The methodology overarching my study is case study, which uses interviews as the primary source of data collection; however, unstructured interviews and oral history interviews are used as well.

Feminist Case Study

> Theory must remain at best hypothetical, at worst unreal and barren [unless we have detailed] case studies and surveys dealing with the experience of selected groups of women in diverse cultures and time periods. (Carroll, 1976, p. xii)

The purpose for undertaking a feminist case study stems out of the historical marginalization and exclusion of women from research. Its aim is also to bring the voices and experiences of women whose stories have not been told or have been told incorrectly to the forefront. As Reinharz states, "Feminist interest in case studies (as in other research formats) stems from a desire to rectify research tainted by gynopia, misogyny, and male-dominated theorizing. Gynopia is the inability to perceive the very existence of women or to perceive women in undistorted ways; misogyny is the hatred of women; and male-dominant theorizing is the creation of theories that assert the superiority of males " (1992, p. 168). She also states that one of the goals of feminist case studies is to "challenge feminists' blindness about particular settings" (p.171). I would expand this goal to include blindness about particular stories and circumstances. This is my desire as I seek to bring the life stories of female adolescent prostitutes to the various feminist theories on prostitution. Although feminist research has been conducted on prostitution, much needs to be explored on adolescent females who fall outside of existing Marxist, liberal, radical, and feminist theoretical frameworks on sex work.

Research Methods

Interview. The primary function of the interview is to provide the researcher with participants' perspectives on the particular phenomenon of interest. It may also serve the function of giving participants a "voice" in research that is conducted about them; "voice" meaning an opinion, an opportunity to be heard. The notion of allowing participants to speak for themselves is critical to both feminist theory and feminist research methodology, as the point of both is to empower women to speak for and about themselves without being censored or misrepresented in ways that are exclusive, exploitive, or oppressive of them:

> Feminist researchers find interviewing appealing for reasons over and above the assets noted by social scientists who defend qualitative methods against positivist criticism. For one thing, interviewing offers researchers access to people's ideas, thoughts, and memories in their own words rather than in the words of the researcher. This asset is particularly important for the study of women because in this way learning from women is an antidote to centuries of ignoring women's ideas altogether or having men speak for women. (Reinharz, 1992, p. 19)

Therefore, offering an opportunity for the voices of women to be heard through interviewing is key to researchers using qualitative feminist research methodology or feminist theory, because inherent in both of these is a need for the space of women's thoughts and experiences. For someone conducting research on such an exploited group as female adolescent dropouts, it is very important that these young women have the opportunity to be heard rather than represented by the thoughts and ideals of the researcher. Belenky et al. state that interviews are very important; especially for women who are even more marginalized, such as minorities, the poor, or exploited groups such as prostitutes:

> ...because we wanted to hear what the women had to say in their own terms rather than test our own preconceived hypotheses, particularly since we included a number of disadvantaged and forgotten women whose ways of knowing and learning, identity transformations, and moral outlook have seldom been examined by academic researchers. We proceeded inductively, opening our ears to the voices and perspective of women so that we might begin to hear the unheard and unimagined....We tried to pose questions that were broad but understandable on may levels, hoping that all—

even less articulate and reflective women—would respond in their own terms without
feeling inadequate to the task. (1986, p. 11)

In keeping with the feminist theoretical framework outlined in this study,
the unstructured and non-directive techniques were used; as noted above,
Reinharz states, "Feminist researchers find interviewing appealing...for one
thing, interviewing offers researchers access to people's ideas, thoughts, and
memories in their own words rather than in the words of the researcher."
Thus, it gives volume to the voices or marginalized people such as the cases
being studied here. Furthermore, if a non-directive style of interviewing is
used, the participants may feel more comfortable expressing their thoughts
instead of telling the researcher what they think is expected. In essence, as
Cohen and Manion state, "It [the non-directive interview method] has been
shown to be a particularly valuable technique because it gets at the deeper
attitudes and perceptions of the person being interviewed in such a way as to
leave them free from interviewer bias" (1989, p.324). The unstructured
interview was used during the initial contact with the participants. An
interview guide was used, but the questions were open-ended, thus allowing
for more freedom of expression from the participants. Successive, non-
directive, in-depth interviews that are characteristic of case study and
ethnography took place later, as the researcher was interested in allowing the
participants to tell their stories.

Oral History

Oral history is an offspring of biographical methodology. Biography as a
methodology is the life experience of someone as told to a researcher. Since
biography has its roots in history, documents and archival records are also
used. Denzin describes biographical methodology as, "the studied use and
collection of life documents that describe turning-point moments in an
individual's life" (1989a, p.69). The tenet that biography and oral history share
is the telling of the life story by a participant to the researcher. They part on
the issue of collecting documents and records, because oral history is defined
as "an approach in which the researcher gathers personal recollections of
events, their causes, and their effects from an individual or several individuals"

(Creswell, 1997, p.49). Thus, oral history seems to add the more explicit element of interpretation by the participant about his or her life experiences. To this end, biographical methodology is more or less interpreted by the researcher; whereas, oral history is interpreted by the participant, though not necessarily entirely.

There are different reasons for a researcher's decision to use the oral history methodology. According to Denzin (1989a), oral history can be used to explore participants' recollection of their life events; hence, it can be used to explore any subject. Feminist oral historians have more specific purposes for using the methodology, stemming from the sociopolitical. Cole (1994), however, posits that when there is a social or political purpose, the researcher is using the life history methodology. "Life history, is an approach...where a researcher reports on an individual's life and how it reflects cultural themes of the society, personal themes, institutional themes, and social histories." The three social justice goals of feminist researchers using oral history methodology are (1) to correct the historical record that omits women due to the fact that men were the subject of most historical accounts, (2) to give voice to women who are already marginalized or who would never get a chance to tell their stories otherwise, and (3) to form a sisterhood between women who are not from the socioeconomic class as the women who are the subject of the oral history (Reinharz, 1992). Therefore, feminist oral history has social justice as its agenda or purpose.

Participants

The study was conducted in Chicago, Illinois. The data collection period lasted three months. Participants included three female adults who entered prostitution as adolescents. Pseudonyms were used to maintain the anonymity of the participants. They were asked to recount their in-school and out-of-school educational experiences. The ages of the participants were 18, 24, and 25. Though one of the original objectives of this study was to cull the perspectives of young women from different races/ethnicities and socioeconomic backgrounds, all of the participants were African American.

Recruitment and Access

As a member of an organization that focuses on addressing the needs of prostitutes, I met other members who provide various services to prostitutes. Through collaboration with other members, I was invited to place flyers on their bulletin boards and introduce the study to the women to ascertain if they would be interested in participating. Two women were recruited and one was referred by another participant. The participants and I then arranged our next meetings, which took place in their residences, bookstores, and restaurants.

Data Collection

Data were collected by taking notes during interviews, as well as through recording the interviews. Both audiotapes and field notes were used ensure the accuracy of the accounts. Immediately following the collection of the data, the researcher wrote journal entries. The audiotapes were transcribed after the data collection was completed. All data, including audiotapes, field notes, journals, consent forms, and so forth were stored in a locked file cabinet in the researcher's place of residence.

Data Analysis

Data analysis began upon collection of the data and continued throughout the data collection process. The data was coded and organized, seeking patterns and themes within each case and across cases. The interviews were transcribed after the data collection was complete. Field notes and journal notes were compared to the interview transcripts to confirm the accuracy of the data. Due to the sensitive nature of the study (IRB considers the research population to be sensitive), observations were not conducted, artifacts were not collected from participants, and family members were not contacted. Therefore, triangulation of the data was an issue. However, I conducted member checks with the participants who were able to be contacted.

Lastly, to the young women (who have to remain nameless) who welcomed me into their lives and made this work possible, thank you for your time, honesty, and patience. God bless you!

I owe so much to my friends and family who supported me through this entire journey: My brothers James and Stephen, the other two-thirds of the big three, who have been my anchors throughout my life; I thank God everyday for them. I am indebted to my aunts who are my othermothers, Hazel Buner, Mildred Cole, Fannie Cole Clark, Garnetta Jackson and Dorothy Nichols, for shouldering my mother's mantle; I'm sure she is grateful. Also, much love and appreciation to Nannette Banks, who was an ear in times of need. I don't think I could have made it without her encouragement and support. Thanks to my friends who went through the doctoral program with me and were my support system, Dr. Pauline Clardy and Dr. Gregory Michie; especially Pauline, who has been a gem to me. I appreciated the company along the journey and strong and undying support.

Many thanks to Dr. Annette Henry, Dr. William Schubert, Dr. William Watkins, Dr. William Ayers and Dr. Audrey Watkins. Dr. Henry has been an excellent mentor and guiding light to me. She opened my mind to a world that was beyond me and introduced me to a body of literature that has become a home to me. All of her work has been tremendously appreciated. Dr. Watkins encouraged me to apply to this doctoral program when a doctorate was the farthest thing from my mind; the many laughs and encouragement will be remembered. Thanks to Bill Ayers for all of your support and guidance as I composed this manuscript.

I am grateful for National-Louis University for the opportunity to grow in my craft. To my department members, especially Jerry Ligon, Marilyn Bizar, Harvey (Smokey) Daniels, Harry Ross, Marilyn Halliday, Anna Silberg, and Scott Sullivan, thanks for all of your collegiality and support.

Much love and thanks to Daniel Martinez, without his help this work would not have been possible.

I have great admiration and appreciation for the teachers who supported and encouraged me through my elementary and secondary schooling: Ms. Jackson, Ms. Johnson, and Mrs. Dorothy Ousley. It is because of them and the difference they have made in my life that I have decided to answer the call to teach.

Lastly, to the young women (who have to remain nameless) who welcomed me into their lives and made this work possible, thank you for your time, honesty, and patience. God bless you!

Forgotten: A Poem

I am in the room, but you don't see me
I answer when you call, yet you don't hear me
I yell STOP, but no one heeds me
I am here, but you don't even know my name.

Sometimes I smile, but it's a polite smile
Sometimes I try, but it's in vain
Sometimes I cry, but not in joy, in pain
I have feelings, but you don't even know my name.

I want to be more, but I don't know how
I want help, but I don't know exactly what to ask for
I want out, but I don't know where to go
Do you remember, do you remember my name?

Cynthia Cole Robinson

Part One

Setting the Backdrop

CHAPTER ONE

Female Dropouts and Prostitution

There is a misconception that dropouts are predominantly male; however, females drop out at approximately the same rate as males (Kaufman et al., 2000; EDC, 1990; Earle & Roach, 1989). While the reasons for dropping out for males and females are similar, the reasons for girls dropping out tend to hinge more on stereotypical roles that socialize them to be caretakers in their home environments and to be less assertive in school settings (Jordan et al., 1994; Baca et al., 1989; Earle & Roach, 1989). These factors lead to females' withdrawals from school.

The issues of female dropouts are important to the study of female adolescent prostitutes, as the vast majority of these young women are dropouts and state that they turn to prostitution as an employment option because they have little schooling and thus few viable economic options (Seng, 1989; Weisberg, 1985; Schaffer & DeBlassie, 1984).

Although research on female dropouts is limited, there are researchers who have either focused solely on the female dropout phenomenon or who have conducted research on males and females but have included gender differences in their data collection and analysis. These researchers may problematize the female dropout phenomenon in various ways, but I synthesize the literature in terms of "push out" and "pull out" factors (Rumberger, 1987; Wehlage & Rutter, 1986). "Push out" factors can be defined as influences that are found within the school environment itself, such as interactions in the classroom with teachers and classmates, the administration, the in-school curriculum, extracurricular activities, and so forth. Hence, push out factors are connected with the in-school curriculum.

"Pull out" factors, in contrast, can be defined as influences found outside of the school environment. They include, but are not limited to, interactions with peers, family, community, media, and so on. Therefore, pull out factors are closely related to the out-of-school curriculum, since it is defined as what is learned in the out-of-school social environment.[4]

Push Out Factors

As I mentioned earlier, push out factors refer to interactions within the school environment that lead to a student withdrawing from school. These interactions can be between teachers and students, the administration, the in-school curriculum, or extracurricular activities. Earle and Roach's report on female dropouts is a direct contradiction of the popular stereotypes claiming that girls drop out less frequently than boys, and that those who do are pregnant. According to Earle and Roach (1989), this is a misconception and, in fact, girls drop out at the same rate as boys. Furthermore, among girls who do leave school, only 40% leave due to pregnancy or marriage; the majority (60%) leave for other reasons.[5] That leaves a huge gap in the literature on female dropouts.

According to Earle and Roach, the predictors for dropouts (both male and female), are socioeconomic status, minority status, and low parental education levels. Predictors that are specific to females are low parental educational levels and a large numbers of siblings. However, Earle and Roach find factors that lead to girls dropping out are based on the gender roles that society constructs for females and males. These gender-based social structures are reflected in schools and affect female dropout rates. The push out factors that affect girls' in-school experience are: (1) the gender-specific socialization of girls, (2) unaddressed cognitive or learning differences of girls, (3) lack of attention or encouragement from teachers, and (4) curricular choices by girls into traditional female courses which lead to underpaying jobs.

Gender-Specific Socialization

This theory reflects the issues and concerns set forth by feminist theory as it is argued that girls are socialized to be noncompetitive, nonassertive, nonaggressive, and cooperative. While they are being socialized to "be quiet and obey", boys are socialized to more forward and exhibit aggressive behaviors. They are taught to be individuals who are competitive and outspoken. These behaviors are rewarded by society, both in the classroom and in the larger world; therefore, they are more prepared to succeed in this competitive society. On the other hand, while boys are taught assertive behaviors that lead to an empowering economic future, girls are rewarded for interpersonal skills that have little relation to academic success and empowering careers. Therefore, boys are prepared for more prestigious careers and to be leaders, while girls are prepared for more service-oriented careers or jobs. Fine's study of dropouts, *Framing Dropouts* (1986), does not focus on gender differences, but she argues that gender discrimination is present in the way in which girls are treated in schools and in classrooms by teachers, and in the larger society as these young women without high school diplomas attempt to navigate through a job market which has little tolerance for the un(der)educated and un(der)skilled (Fine, 1992; Fine & Zane, 1989).

Learning Differences

Because of the manner in which girls are taught to behave and conduct themselves (to work in groups, to be considerate of others, to find commonalities among peers), the classroom environment in which they thrive is one of cooperative learning. However, most classrooms are structured for individual learning; lecture is the pedagogical tool of choice, and it calls for individual responses (Sadker & Sadker, 1994). This is to girls' disadvantage because it suits the learning patterns of boys (individual, competitive, and desiring to stand out from the group), while ignoring the learning styles of girls (Horgan, 1995; Yates, 1993).

Teacher Interaction

Teachers tend to interact more with boys in the classroom (Sadker & Sadker, 1995; Yates, 1993). They spend more time showing boys how to complete assignments and tasks; thus, encouraging them to become proficient performing those tasks independently. However, they are more likely to complete tasks for girls, leaving them dependent and unable to complete those tasks on their own. Teacher attention is related to academic achievement. Teachers are more likely to praise boys for their actual academic performance and reprimand them for stylistics like handwriting. The opposite is true of their interactions with girls (reprimanded for academic performance and praised for stylistics). As a result, girls tend to have low self-esteem as it relates to their academic ability, while boys are reinforced in a way that leads to confidence in academic ability.

The Women's Educational Equity Act Program (WEEAP) also found that gender-based differences in schools are also considered to be a key factor in girls dropping out. Gender biases exist in the way in which classrooms are structured and in the interactions between teachers and students (McCormick, 1994; Earle & Roach, 1989). The pedagogical practices of teachers, for the most part, consist of practices that accommodate boys' learning styles rather than girls' (WEEAP, 1990). Lecturing and individualized instruction cater to the way in which boys are socialized to be aggressive, assertive, and competitive. Group activities are less a part of teachers' pedagogical practices, though these practices are better suited for girls, who are socialized to be cooperative and collaborative (McCormick, 1994; Earle & Roach, 1989). Furthermore, while student achievement is directly related to the amount of attention given by the teacher, girls receive less teacher attention (Horgan, 1995; McCormick, 1994). However, research shows that teachers tend to give boys more attention due to their more aggressive socialization as opposed to girls who are socialized to be quiet. As a result, girls get less attention from teachers, while boys are given a great deal. Researchers posit that this lack of attention and feedback from teachers leads to self-esteem issues for girls and create a "learned helplessness" contributing to academic failure and eventually dropping out.

Curricular Decisions

Girls are not encouraged to take courses that are considered to be traditionally "male" such as math and science. In fact, they are dissuaded from taking those types of courses. This is problematic since many of the professions in these areas are higher-paying jobs. Instead, girls are over-represented in the type of vocational jobs that prepare them for the service industry, such as cosmetology, nursing, etc.

Maladjustment to the School Environment

This factor is directly involved with the school, such as not liking school, conflictual relationships with teachers, feeling disconnected from or not belonging in the school environment, falling behind in school work, and failing in school (such as classes and grade retention). When these factors are at issue, Jordan et al. (1994) posit that it negatively affects the connection that students make with school in general and causes them to "reject the context of schooling". This rejection then leads to acting out in school or behavior problems, frequent absences, and a lack of academic effort. Schools, in return, respond to the behavior with failing grades, retention, suspension, and/or expulsion. This exacerbates the problem, pushing them towards dropping out.

Socioeconomic Factors

In the past, research on dropouts echoed the stereotypes that depicted them as lazy, voiceless adolescents of low intellectual ability who were disinterested and disenchanted by education (Tidwell, 1988; Cervantes, 1965; Sewell, Palmo, & Manni, 1981). They were typified as psychologically depressed, with little hope or thought for themselves and the future. Fine's critical response to this depiction was her research on dropouts. In her study, she delved deeper into their experiences, both as students and as people living real lives and interacting with the real world. Fine posited that many educational institutions do not respond to or realize students' lived realities.

In *Framing Dropouts*, she examined the dropout phenomenon using an ethnographic approach, as she immersed herself into the daily operations of Central High School, a comprehensive or general-education high school in New York City, and in the out-of-school lives of these students. She looked at the dropout issue from a myriad of perspectives: the administrators, the teachers, the parents, and the dropouts. Her findings were that the educational system actually works against dropouts, who could be more accurately termed "push outs."   Furthermore, these former students are wrongly portrayed and victimized by a system that does not want to hear their critical voices or deal with the real-life problems that they bring into the classrooms. Her theory on dropouts can best be summarized as: (1) silencing of critical voices and consciousness of students—the school doesn't address issues of racism, sexism, and classism   (even with those who do obtain degrees); (2) equal education access, but unequal outcomes—while public education is mandated up to age 16, the level and type of education is far from equal, and with much of school funding relying on income taxes, rich students have access to a higher-quality education; (3) economic "bottom-lining"—since schools only receive funds for those who attend school for a specified amount of days a year, those on the fringes of dropping out (who are truants) are seen as a liability and financial drain; and (4) reproduction of social classes (with the minority poor as permanent occupants of the bottom rung)—poor students are taught to go along with a system that already oppresses them and trains them to be in service industries, as Anyon (1996) finds in her study of how school curricula reproduces social classes. In their study of male and female dropouts, Baca et al. (1989) also found that social class had a great impact on school dropout rates as they found that poverty and racial/ethnic background were predictors for dropping out, as poor minority girls had a higher noncompletion rate than White girls; thus reflecting that minority females face issues stemming from racial, socioeconomic, and gender inequity, as Black feminist theorists posit (Collins, 1990).

The WEEAP also examined the female dropout issue from economic and social perspectives. According to their research and theory, women who drop out have a difficult time finding employment in this society—which is rapidly and continuously becoming more skills-oriented and technologically based. With female dropouts being unskilled, it makes it extremely difficult for them to find any employment, much less gainful employment. As they state, female dropouts who are employed earn only 40% of what high school graduates earn. Therefore, the result of noncompletion for females is devastating, as women are the head of over half of poverty-stricken households (WEEAP, 1990). This is a vicious cycle for the female dropout, as girls from poor homes are at an increased risk for noncompletion. This poverty determinant is exacerbated for minority females, as being a minority and poor raises the chances of dropping out. Thus, lack of education and racial discrimination makes it impossible for minority female dropouts to evade a life of poverty.

Baca et al.'s (1989) study covers several aspects of the female dropout phenomenon, from school-related factors to personal factors. They found that school-related factors played a key role in girls' decisions to drop out. While falling behind in schoolwork was the strongest indicator, the issues that lead to this come from a myriad of sources. These sources are high absenteeism, illness, failure to do homework, responsibilities of parenthood, and frequent changing of schools, among others. It is unclear as to why these girls are absent, sick, or don't do schoolwork; however, it is clear that these things are a result of issues that girls face outside of school, such as having to care for other siblings in the case of girls who come from large families. These indicators are frequently found among low-income and minority girls, as there is often a lack of parental support and/or supervision in their home environments. Many were found to have low self-esteem and low confidence, as is commonly found among female dropouts. These issues may stem from factors outside of the school; however, the researchers state that it is the school's duty to assist with counteracting them by implementing programs (counseling, tutoring, and mentoring) and establishing relationships with outside social service agencies.

Pull Out Factors

Pull out factors refer to those interactions and influences outside of the school environment that affect students' decisions to dropout. The most commonly cited pull out factors for girls are socioeconomic in nature, which may result from responsibilities placed on them due to the fact that they are girls and are socialized to be caretakers.

Family Related

Issues in the family were found to be a key reason that girls dropped out of school, reflecting feminist theorists' assertions that females are still socialized into care-taking roles and are expected to make career, educational, and professional goals secondary (Omolade, 1994). While the family-related problems vary (whether it be a pregnant, sick, drug-dependent, or hard-working parent, working too much to care for their family adequately) they all seem to lead to the issue of females being forced to take on the traditional female role of caretaker in the home. Although Fine's study is not focused on gender differences in the dropout rate, she does state that she found girls were more likely to drop out because of family-related issues such as pregnancy or having to care for siblings or for an ailing parent (Fine, 1986). As a result of this surrogate duty, many girls feel compelled to miss school to tend to the needs of the family. That could range from staying home to baby-sit siblings that are not of school age, taking a job to help out financially (which could conflict with school schedules or leave them too exhausted to attend school), to nursing an ill parent. Thus, overwhelming need by the family pulls these young women out of school.

Job Related

Many times, the need to have a job stems from the family's need for financial support. In these cases, a girl may need to support her child, herself, and/or a parent. This becomes an issue as many jobs conflict with the school schedule or entail responsibilities that are too overwhelming when added to the responsibilities of school. This seems to be an accurate assertion, as 63% of those working reported that they couldn't work and go to school at the same time (Jordan et al., 1994). Girls who drop out make the decision that supplying pressing financial needs is more important than school, which many are disenchanted with anyway.

Dropping Out and the Adolescent Female Prostitute

The aforementioned theories on dropping out, particularly those of Baca et al. (1989) and Jordan et al. (1994), state that withdrawal from school does not result from one event or problem, but that it is often an interaction of many events or problems, whether it is falling behind in school, family problems, etc. While research on adolescent prostitutes has not focused on the school history of these girls, the research studies indicate that the predicators for dropping out are present in the lives of female adolescent prostitutes, as many state that they were having problems at home and needed to leave or needed to help out financially, and that they felt alienated at school (Schaffer & DeBlassie, 1984; Silbert & Pines, 1982; Enablers, 1978; Gray, 1973). Just as dropping out results from a number of factors, the transition into adolescent prostitution is a product of many issues. Thus, adolescent prostitution lies at the intersection of sociological, economic, and psychological issues, which lead to a limitation of economic options, leaving many girls in financial positions that they feel can only be remedied through prostitution. Since the overwhelming majority of adolescent prostitutes feel that they have to enter and remain in the prostitution industry because they lack the education (most are school dropouts) needed to secure viable work options, the issues that led to their decision to leave school is key to preventing girls who are at risk of falling into that lifestyle, as well as to creating programs in school and alternative education programs to assist these girls in continuing or completing their education.

There is a great deal of research on adolescent prostitution; however, research focused solely on the educational experiences of these girls is needed. Some studies do make brief mention of their school experiences, stating their negative feelings and experiences in school (Weisberg, 1985; Schaffer & DeBlassie, 1984; Fisher et al., 1982; Silbert & Pines, 1982; Enablers, 1978; Gray, 1973). Also, while the reasons they drop out are not examined in these studies, reasons for entering prostitution and information on their social backgrounds are discussed. Interestingly, many of the reasons they give for entering prostitution are the same as the reasons theorists give for girls dropping out. As a result, it is reasonable to hypothesize that these same issues also affected their decisions to drop out.

My emerging theoretical ideas on female adolescent dropout prostitutes are informed by Rumberger (1987) and Wehlage & Rutter's (1986) push out and pull out factors and WEEAP's (1990) theory of poverty and limited career and economic options for female dropouts. Fine's (1986) theory states that dropouts have healthy self-esteem and are less depressed, however that does not hold true to the literature on female adolescent prostitutes. Baca et al. (1989) state that confidence and self-image are not big factors for female dropouts, but the literature on this population of girls shows that self-image has a huge effect on them; thus, their theory does not agree with research findings on my specific population. Therefore, though Jordan's and WEEAP's theories on dropping out do not address all of the factors that may lead to these girls' withdrawal from school, they do address key issues.

Specific Push Out Factors for Adolescent Female Prostitutes

Feeling as though they didn't belong. Research findings on teen prostitutes indicate that many girls who drop out and are in jeopardy of entering prostitution feel disconnected from school because it does not meet their needs or support them: "The teenager who has received little reinforcement within the academic environment is unlikely to place much value on education (Schaffer & DeBlassie, 1984). Ellenwood supports this claim stating,

> Three types of children are "at-risk" for running in the school environment: the successful student who comes to feel overwhelmed or angered by relentless pressure, (b) the child who consistently fails and begins to believe s/he is a misfit, and thus,

tries to escape to save dignity, and (c) the chronically transient child who grows up without friends, and, thus, without a sense of belonging to the school. (1991, p. 4)

Though there is an array of research on prostitution, there is a need for this industry to be researched in terms of the education of prostitutes (education is used widely here in the sense of life education; more traditional forms of education will be referred to as "schooling"): how nonschool curricula (Schubert, 1986) affects entry into the field and maintenance within the industry, why traditional approaches towards life (i.e., schooling and traditional careers) are not pursued, and what school experiences of prostitutes were like. However, research studies show that 50–85% of prostitutes are dropouts, truants (77.8%), and have poor grades (Seng, 1989).

Didn't get along with teachers. Although over half of the girls in the studies reported that they didn't get along with their teachers due to behavior or attitudinal issues, the details of the negative interactions are not discussed (Tidwell, 1988). This is one area that I plan to explore in my study, as indicators show that relationships with teachers have a strong impact on these students' disdain for school and their decisions to drop out.

Specific Pull Out Factors for Adolescent Female Prostitutes

Economic. In both the research of Jordan et al. (1994) and WEEAP (1990), they found that students dropped out to meet financial needs through work. Female adolescent prostitutes also report that finances were a very important factor in dropping out as well as in entering prostitution. However, where Jordan states that many girls drop out to help the family financially, not all female adolescent prostitutes drop out to help the family. In fact, in many cases they report that they are trying to support themselves, not the family, as many leave their home environments to escape abuse:

> In all research, money is mentioned as the prime motive. Jackman et al. (1963) point out that for teenagers, prostitution is a means for obtaining easy money which leads to immediate rewards. Those from lower socioeconomic families find that the money can provide the otherwise unattainable things in life, and with that with money comes a sense of self-importance. (Schaffer & DeBlassie, 1984, p. 691)

In the WEEAP research, they state that female dropouts face economic hardship due to the fact that they are undereducated and that they face gender discrimination. This echoes some of the feminist views of prostitution, "Given the inequitable status of women in society, some feminists have characterized women who work in the sex trade as victims of exploitation and abuse" (Sloan & Wahab, 2000, p. 461). I would agree that this view is valid, that indeed prostitutes are victims of unfortunate circumstances, for the same reasons cited in the article by Wynter (1987):

> ...reject the lie that women freely choose prostitution from a whole array of economic alternatives that exist under civil equity. As I stated..., it is not possible to hold the position that prostitution is a choice when research statistics reveal that many of these young women suffer from, "...high rates of child abuse, wife-battering, rape, poor female-headed households, no equal rights amendment, and inequitable wages, women live with civil inequity that does not allow free choices, especially in regard to potentially life-threatening work. (pp. 268-269)

Teen prostitutes express the same view, as a participant states:

> My major problems were paying my bills and not having anything; I needed a place to live. I had no friends, no money, and no family to rely on. Nobody cares about a young girl who needs money and some help. They force you into prostitution. You have no choice when you got nothing. (Silbert & Pines, 1982, p. 485)

Issues of class are also present in young women's decisions to transition into prostitution; as Silbert & Pines (1982) state, 88% report that they live in extreme poverty.

Family Problems. The majority of adolescent prostitutes are runaways or throwaways, meaning that they were asked or forced to leave their living environments. Many report that they ran away due to sexual, physical, and/or mental abuse that they experienced in their home environment and need the money from prostitution as a means of supporting themselves (Ellenwood, 1991; Chesney-Lind, 1989; Figueria-McDonough, 1985; Weisberg, 1985; Ivers & Carlson, 1987; Bracey, 1983). More in-depth research into reasons why these runaways leave home show that more than 70% of them are sexually abused by someone in their household, typically a father or stepfather. Without the financial support of the home environment, many are faced with finding a means of financial support, and unfortunately, for an overwhelming number of females that source is prostitution. Therefore, entrance into the prostitution industry also seems to be based on other social problems such as dysfunctional home environments.

Adolescent Prostitution

The majority (70-80%) of young women who are involved in prostitution are dropouts.[6] Thus, dropping out of school seems to be related to the transition into prostitution. When young women involved in prostitution are asked why they entered prostitution or why they remain in the industry, they reply that they did not have any other options for reasonable employment based on the fact that they did not have adequate schooling. As Deisher et al. (1982) state, "Social support on the street, stigma and ostracism from their previous communities, financial need and lack of educational and employment experience all inhibit an adolescent's ability to break away from the streets (p. 820). Gray states:

> The teenage prostitute is likely to have quit school voluntarily due to experiences of repeated failure to adjust to the academic setting. As a result of such experience, she does not see education as relevant to her future or as a source of reinforcement for her now or later in her life. Ties to educational values, then, are broken before entry into prostitution and, as does the breaking of home ties, set the stage for the girl's future role as a streetwalker. (1973, p. 406)

As a result of this lack of schooling and hence a lack of gainful employment, many young women find prostitution as their only economic option. Silbert and Pines (1982) found that 88% of their participants viewed prostitution as their only option because they were either too young to be employed or had no education or skills.

Sociological Background

Due to the illegal nature of prostitution and the transience of the population, there is not a comprehensive study that can definitively give the average age of girls entering prostitution; however, individual studies that have focused on adolescents as well as adult prostitutes have found that the average age for entrance into the industry is 16[7] (Schaffer & DeBlassie, 1984; Enablers, 1978; Silbert & Pines, 1982). Research focused on adolescents shows that the average age for them to enter into prostitution is age 13 to 14 (Weisberg, 1985; Schaffer & DeBlassie, 1984; Silbert & Pines, 1982; James & Meyerling, 1977). The fact that young women enter prostitution when they are still school age may be shocking; however, as stated earlier, the majority of adolescent prostitutes are runaways or throwaways, meaning that they were asked or forced to leave their living environments. Many of these young women ran from their living situations because they were subjected to physical, sexual, and or mental abuse. Without the financial support of the home environment, many have to find a way of making a living in order to survive on their own. For many young girls, that means of financial support is prostitution. Therefore, their entrance into prostitution seems to be based on other social problems such as dysfunctional living situation.

Psychological Background

The majority of these young women have experienced some form of physical and mental abuse, which led directly or indirectly to their transition into prostitution.

> In a Minnesota survey of prostitutes under the age of 20, 65% reported being raped as their first sexual experience with intercourse. Only 5% reported that their first experience occurred as a result of incest, but approximately 30% admitted having incurred family sexual abuse; 50% reported the occurrence of family conflict immediately prior to entering prostitution. (Schaffer & DeBlassie, 1984, p. 690)

Silbert and Pines (1982) cite similar rates of abuse, "When presented with a checklist of serious home problems and asked to indicate which of the problems they experienced, 70% of the subjects reported emotional abuse; 62%, physical abuse; and 60% sexual abuse" (p. 484). They also report that 96% of the prostitutes involved in their study were raped and 84% of the rapes did not take place while they were working.

Many have poor self-image due to the abuses that they have suffered:

> When asked what kind of problems they had just before they became
> prostitutes....The most frequently mentioned problems were general psychological,
> emotional problems (68%); for example, "I hated me and everyone else," or "I felt
> crazy and depressed" ....Most of the subjects (94%) felt very negatively about
> themselves prior to starting prostitution. (Silbert & Pines, 1982, p. 485)

These young women have emotional and psychological problems due to
the abuse they suffer prior to and during prostitution. Seng (1989) reports that
of the 35 subjects in her study involved in prostitution, 82.9% were depressed,
77.8% were potentially suicidal, and 85.7% had a poor self-image (p. 669).
However, most of these young women do not receive any form of therapy or
counseling. Furthermore, after entering prostitution, many are sexually
assaulted and/or physically abused and do not receive counseling due to the
fact that, as prostitutes, many health care services do not take their cases
seriously. This implies that the mental and physical well-being of these women
does not matter, and that prostitutes are viewed as undeserving of medical
attention.

Educational Background

As I have previously stated in the sociological section of this literature
review, the majority of adolescent prostitutes are runaways. Due to this fact,
many withdraw from the educational system, as they do not have contact with
anything that is related to the home life that they are leaving. This places the
young women at a disadvantage because they lack even the basic education
needed to obtain more traditional forms of work, even it they saw it as an
option.

In our society, the mainstream view or the "American dream" of life is to
get an education and start a career. This view of life is predicated upon
investing time and effort in the immediate (school) in hopes of benefiting in
the future with a career that will supply a traditional lifestyle. This ideology is
problematic for runaways, many of whom become prostitutes for the lack of
other means of financial support, as Ellenwood (1991) states that, "...runaways

frequently report having rejected traditional social values and established societal values. They see those values as leading to further loneliness and frustration" (p.3). Research on runaways who turn to prostitution shows that they lack the future-orientated frame of thinking needed to endure traditional schooling. Ivers and Carlson state:

> Acquiring academic credentials results for most people in the development of a future-oriented attitude about their life. Juvenile prostitutes with little education have learned, however, to manipulate their environments in hopes of achieving immediate short term rewards at the expense of long term rewards. (1987, p. 3)

This failure to see traditional schooling as a viable possibility raises questions about the educational experiences of these young women such as: How do they view promises of traditional schooling, i.e., career and life opportunities? How do they view school and what was their schooling experience like? What is lacking in schools when prostitution seems to be the only answer for these girls? What prompted them to drop out and lead this alternative life?

As stated earlier in the "push out factors" section, research indicates that many female dropouts who are in jeopardy of becoming prostitutes feel disconnected from school and feel that it does not meet their needs or support them: "The teenager who has received little reinforcement within the academic environment is unlikely to place much value on education" (Schaffer & DeBlassie, 1984, p. 690). What did or didn't they receive from the educational system that leads them to reject the benefits of schooling? Is it possible that their experiences as girls in an educational system that does not address the needs of females affected their decision to withdraw or lose faith in it?

Although there is an array of research on prostitution, there is a need for this industry to be researched in terms of the education of prostitutes.[8] These issues need to be explored: (1) how nonschool curricula (Schubert, 1986) affect entry into the field and maintenance within the industry, (2) why traditional approaches towards life (i.e., schooling and traditional careers) are not pursued, and (3) what school experiences of prostitutes were like. Many prostitutes drop out (45.5%), are truants (77.8%), and have poor grades (50%)

(Seng, 1989). Whereas prostitutes may be viewed by some as uneducated due to the fact that such a large percentage of them have not completed traditional schooling, I would argue that they are highly educated in their knowledge of street life and basic survival skills.

CHAPTER TWO

Feminist Theory and Prostitution

Feminist theory is rooted in what Marx terms "praxis" and Paulo Freire defines as "reflection and action upon the world in order to transform it" (1998, p. 33); it is the fusion between theory and social action. This is key to feminist theory because the pulse of its very theory is social activism; i.e., the changing of the social, political, and economic reality of women. As Humm states:

> The first idea that is likely to occur in the course of any historical thinking about feminism is that feminism is a social force. The emergence of feminist ideas and feminist politics depends on the understanding that, in all societies which divide the sexes into differing cultural, economic or political spheres, women are less valued than men. Feminism also depends on the premise that women can consciously and collectively change their social place. (1992, p. 1)

Thus, in feminist theory we see the marriage of theory to practice or social movement bounded by the political. Therefore, it is dismissive to discuss feminist theory apart from the feminist movement.

Feminist theory grows out of what is known as the feminist movement. The feminist movement can be described in three general patterns, all of which are closely related to or an evolution of its predecessor: first-wave feminism, second-wave feminism, and contemporary feminism. First-wave feminism characterizes a political movement that has its genesis in antislavery efforts of the 1840s Thus, the first wave of feminism was concerned with political equality and the legal rights of women.

Second-wave feminism, like first-wave feminism, was also a product of the social and political times, building on issues of reproductive rights, the unique experiences of women, and equality. This age of feminism stems from the civil rights movement led by African Americans regarding equal treatment and equal opportunities for Blacks. As Evans (1995) posits, this wave of feminism was about equality with men in lieu of our differences: "Then the notion of 'equality in difference' enters in. (This is the idea that we merit equal though not identical treatment; equal in the sense of 'equally good, and more appropriate to us.')" (p. 3).

Off the cuffs of second-wave feminism grew the need for differences among women to be explored. Some women began to claim that feminism did not suit the purposes of all women, that in fact it had a very specific group of women in mind: middle-class, White, heterosexual women (Collins, 1990; hooks, 1981, 1984; Lorde, 1984). Thus, the exclusionary aspects of second-wave feminism came to bear. From the failure of White, mainstream, second-wave feminism came contemporary feminism, which recognizes the plurality of women and their various social plights. It is concerned with differences; issues of race, ethnicity, class, sexuality, language, and disability make it impossible for there to be one "woman experience," but that there are multiple experiences of being a woman. Hence, Black feminism emerged and was among the first to voice this need of expanding feminism.

Although there are various schools of feminist thought, these voices of dissension have been key in forming feminisms that address the issues and concerns of women from a myriad of social, economic, and racial backgrounds. These different schools of thought have made it possible for feminist theory to include multiple perspectives.

There is much difference among feminists and these various schools of thought; however, there are some basic goals or agenda that all have in common. It is these general posts of feminist theory that makes it a tool of liberation for women: (1) to liberate women from patriarchal oppression through praxis, (2) to validate and make known the experiences of women and to give them voice, and (3) "equality in difference" by extending rights.

Prostitution and Feminist Theory

Prostitution is an activity whose origins can be traced over the centuries. It is an age-old occupation that is typically identified as female and carries with it a social stigma that still exists today. When many people think of a prostitute, the image that comes to mind may be the one that is popularized by the media of a forward, aggressive, confident, scantily clad adult woman who is on the prowl and enjoys the occupation-turned-lifestyle that she has "chosen". I emphasize chosen because it is a stereotypical misconception among many that prostitution is a choice that women make; however, the sociological, psychological, and educational factors that contribute to the transition into this lifestyle are not considered. More than half of the women involved in prostitution have been sexually and physically abused, are from dysfunctional families (which is the nucleus of many other social and psychological problems), and are school dropouts (Brown, 1979; Nagle, 1997).[9] Another misconception is that all prostitutes are female and adults, when the research indicates that most prostitutes enter the lifestyle at age 14 (Schaffer, 1984; Enablers, 1978). Whereas prostitution is viewed as a "chosen" adult activity, it is first an issue of exploited and victimized adolescents. Research has shown that a disproportionate amount of female prostitutes are runaways or throwaways (those who were requested to leave their living environments) and have been sexually abused, many by relatives (Calhoun et al., 1993; Ellenwood, 1991; Ivers & Carlson, 1987). Furthermore, a great number of prostitutes are from lower to lower-middle class families headed by single parents with little education or economical viability (Seng, 1989; Weisberg, 1985). The societal norm for a preteen and a teenager is the life of a student preparing for secondary and post-secondary education; however, these teens are far from "normal" and are living lives to which most adults can not relate. While society may view prostitution as an adult issue, it truly is an adolescent issue that has matured into what is misconceived as an adult issue. Therefore, prostitution as a lifestyle is not a responsible, informed, adult choice at all, but an attempt at survival for many victimized children.[10]

Only within the past 15 years has prostitution been given attention as an activity that begins during the adolescent years (Brock, 1998). Although it is primarily a female activity, feminism only has begun to address the issue in terms of social inequity and economic injustice in the 1990s. The perspectives on the issue range from the conservative perspective of prostitution as a hindrance to the women's movement, morally corrupt, and a chosen activity to the radical perspective that it is a form of sexual empowerment (Sloan & Wahab, 2000). These various feminist perspectives generally don't address the fact that prostitution is an adolescent issue affected by many social and psychological problems. Inherent in these views is the idea that "prostitution is a choice". Therefore, both views forego the notion that prostitution cannot be a choice since entrance into the industry has been documented at approximately 14 years of age. Thus, they are children and cannot be regarded as capable of making such a decision. There are those within the movement, such as Black feminists, who deal with issues of marginalization of women of varied races, ethnicities, and classes by mainstream or White feminists; however, they do not address the uniqueness of the position of the prostitute or the social and psychological issues that she faces (Collins, 1990). However, research does validate the position of Black feminists in that it shows that even within the prostitution industry, Black women face racial discrimination: "The situation is worse for women of color in the sex industry, who often face stereotyping as the Jezebel or the Exotic Other in addition to pervasive racism and sexism in our culture" (Guidroz, 1996). Thus, Black prostitutes suffer the same social problems as do Black women in more traditional occupations. They are victimized by their clients, who want to enact strange fantasies and fetishes perpetuated by society about Black women. Thus, the experiences of Black prostitutes vary from those of White prostitutes, as this conversation among two Black sex workers shows:

> ML: In this [sex work] industry, it is very hard to be your ethnic self if it doesn't sell.
> GL: I think that in the industry, regardless of what it is, people are in it for fantasies and what they want is what everybody else wants, which, unfortunately, is tall, blonde, big-busted women with long hair.
> ML: I find my Blackness beautiful, but ironically, I don't enjoy it when clients

eroticize it. I get all these guys who just want me to put my hands on my hips, crack gum, and speak with a ghetto dialect.

GL: The tricks, who were mostly White, as most of our customers have always been White. Even though they like Black women, they still didn't want us to be Black. They wanted us to be something else. They wanted to believe that we were Pocahontas. (Nagle, 1997, p.199–200)

There is a myriad of feminist theories on prostitution; they span from the view that prostitutes are victims to the view that they are sexually liberated and are socially stigmatized. Given the inequitable status of women in society, some feminists have characterized women who work in the sex trade as victims of exploitation and abuse and believe the commercial exchange of sex should be abolished (Russell, 1993; Wynter, 1987; Dworkin, 1987; Barry, 1979). Other feminists, however, believe that despite the lack of equity between men and women, sex work is a legitimate profession stigmatized by a sexually repressed society, such as organizations including current and former prostitutes like Call Off Your Tired Old Ethics (COYOTE) and Hooking Is Real Employment, HIRE (Sloan & Wahab, 2000).

Issues of class are also present in young women's decisions to transition into prostitution; as Silbert and Pines (1982) state, 88% report that they live in extreme poverty. This may appear ironic due to the amount of money prostitutes make on the streets; however, they rarely benefit economically from their work because many are employed by pimps who mandate the release of all profits to him. If they fail to do so or are suspected of withholding some of their profits, they are physically abused (Bracey, 1982). This is just one more way in which men exploit these women.

Feminist Theories on Prostitution

In this section, various feminist theories on prostitution will be examined. The perspectives on prostitution range from the notion that it oppresses and exploits women, to the view that it is empowers them because it allows them to charge men for what they expect to receive for free. Although the views vary greatly, one fact remains: women seeking to earn a wage use prostitution as a form of labor. Thus, prostitution, as an industry, is definitely driven by economics. The feminist perspectives on prostitution that will be covered are Marxist feminism, domination theory, Black feminist thought, liberal feminism, radical sexual pluralist theory feminism, and sex worker feminism.

Marxist feminists: The Marxist perspective of feminism examines prostitution as a result of capitalism. In a society where class structure exists, there will be a ruling class and a laboring class. Hence, the ruling class is in a position to exploit the working class. According to Marxist theory, those who are exploited or at the bottom of this social order are proletariats or persons who exchange their labor for a wage. Thus, when the worker is no longer able to labor, there is no more wage, as Carolyn Steedman states, "...all you have in the end is your labour" (Steedman, 1986, p. 43). In classical Marxist theory, this labor is usually one of the hands and not of the mind, as proletarian work is typically alienating and of an automaton-like nature which can be done by anyone. As a result, the worker is dehumanized, while the profit of his or her labor is given to the ruling class. This theory applies to prostitution in that the prostitute's labor is sex work. Her body becomes commodified and sex becomes the commodity, leading to her exploitation:

> Just as the capacity to labor becomes a commodity under capitalism, so does sexuality, especially the sexuality of women. Thus prostitutes, like waging laborers, having an essential human capacity alienated. Like wage laborers, they become dehumanized and their value as persons is measured by their market price. And like wage laborers, they are compelled to work by economic pressure; prostitution, if not marriage, may well be the best option available to them. (Jaggar, 1991, p. 375)

Thus, prostitutes are exploited by the ruling class, which could be considered the patriarchy, and more specifically by the pimp since he receives the direct profit of her labor. In fact, Marx likens the state of the prostitute to that of the proletariat worker when he proclaims, "Prostitution is only the specific expression of the universal, prostitution of the worker" (Marx, 1975, p.350). Prostitution for Marxist feminists, then, is a metaphor for the oppression of the wage laborer in the capitalist system.

Though Marxist feminists account for issues of class in their theory, they equate the socioeconomic position of prostitutes to that of the wage laborer, which bypasses gender issues. Though wage laborers are exploited by the ruling class, prostitutes are further exploited by the ruling class and by men (there are also male prostitutes, but the industry remains predominantly female).

Domination-theory feminists: Domination theory holds the view that the root of women's oppression rests in sexuality. It suggests that prostitution is not an industry, but that it is the state in which all women find themselves. The argument is that the sexuality of women is reliant on their objectification by men, "Women's sexuality is, socially, a thing to be stolen, sold, bought, bartered, or exchanged by others [those others being males]....Women never own or possess it" (MacKinnon, 1987, p.58). Therefore, women are always victims of male sexual desire.

Domination-theory feminists believe that prostitution is not a choice by women and that it has nothing to do with women's desire, because in their view sex work is oppressive. "In fact domination theory assumes the radical feminist position (see Dworkin, 1987; Jaggar, 1991; Zatz, 1997) that sex work is inherently oppressive and violent and serves the purpose of asserting male dominance and power over women" (Sloan & Wahab, 2000, p.463). In fact, they posit that the very physical act of sexual intercourse is violent and victimizes women:

> There is never a real privacy of the body that can coexist with intercourse: with being entered. The vagina itself is a muscle and the muscles have to be pushed apart. The thrusting is persistent invasion. She is opened up, split down the center. She is occupied-physically, internally, in her privacy....Violation is a synonym for intercourse. (Dworkin, 1987, p. 122)

Because prostitution and other sex work are reliant upon men as the client and in many cases as the broker, i.e., the pimp, it is regarded as one of the highest forms of female exploitation. In fact, many of these theorists refer to prostitution as the female sexual slave trade (Cole, 1987; Barry 1979).

The problems that are raised within domination theory are manifold: (1) it has as its core tenet women's objectification by male sexual desire and it rejects the notion that men can be prostitutes. This is problematic because it is a fact that there are male prostitutes, and in the case of homosexual relationships other men can be, and often are, the object of men's desire; (2) it suggests that women are victims of sex in general, as Dworkin states that, "violation is a synonym for sex" (p.122); and (3) it overstates prostitution as a condition that plagues all women by claiming that all women share the same social stigma as prostitutes (MacKinnon, 1983). Therefore, the circumstances and issues that actual prostitutes face are overshadowed by this generalization.

Liberal feminists on sex work: The liberal feminist perspective of prostitution varies between those who argue that sex work is degrading and those who believe that it is the same as any other labor that workers perform to earn a wage. The common stance for both is that sex work should be legalized. The tenet behind this position is that the criminalization of prostitution denies the sex workers the right to make decisions regarding their own bodies. The line of reasoning follows the same one set forth by *Roe v. Wade*: women should have the right to control what they do with their bodies. "According to the American Civil Liberties Union, laws that prohibit prostitution are unconstitutional on the grounds that they interfere with individuals' right to control their bodies and deny women equal protection under the law" (Sloan & Wahab, 2000). Both camps also agree that prostitution is anchored in the lack of economic opportunities and resources for women. As a result, prostitution grows out of the oppression that women face in this patriarchal society.

The liberal feminist strand begins to splinter on the issue of the degradation of women. According to what I will term as conservative-liberal feminism, sex work is degrading. It is particularly degrading because women sell their bodies in exchange for money. Thus, women are objectified and the selling of any woman sends the message that all women are goods to be purchased at the will of men.

The liberal feminists argue that the selling of sex is no different than the selling of other types of labor in exchange for a wage, "...sex work is a social contract in which the sex worker contracts out a service for a certain amount of time and is a free worker just like any other wage laborer" (Jaggar, 1991). Thus, sex work for liberal feminists is the selling of a service, similar to the service a woman who works in a dry cleaner provides. This is a capitalist perspective of work, since Marx argues that no wage laborer is ever free in a capitalist system, for they must labor in order to survive. This, in and of itself, makes the wage laborer a slave to labor.

Radical sexual-pluralist theory: Radical sexual-pluralist theory was developed by Rubin as an opposition to binaries and grand theories on sexuality. It posits that sexuality should not be divided into categories of good and bad, normal and deviant. To make these distinctions based on what one group's notion of what acceptable sexual behavior or relations are is to marginalize those who fall outside of those boundaries. Thus, she constructs an argument that is similar to that of Black feminists, as she harkens to the plight of "otherness".[11] Central to this theory is the notion that:

> ...no sexual behavior is more moral than any other and that privileging one sexuality over others creates an illusion that there is only one best way to do things—a type of thinking that is seen as dangerous in that it perpetuates a system of sexual judgment that dichotomizes sexual acts into good and bad, normal and abnormal, natural and unnatural. (Sloan & Wahab, 2000, p. 470)

The product of constructing such binarisms is that the dominant thinking is heralded, while the "others" considered deviant are condemned. This is seen in the case of prostitutes and other sex workers. They are viewed as a plague on society that should be cured or eradicated.

Rubin instead suggests that sex workers not be marginalized, but that they should speak out against their marginalization. Also, she suggests that theorists begin to take sex workers' experiences into account and that they make space for their voices to be heard. It is the position of this theory that sex work be legitimized, as are traditional forms of work, that prostitution be legalized in the cases where it occurs between to consenting adults, and that the image of sex workers as victims of exploitation and oppression be reworked to depict them as political and sexual figures.

Sex workers on sex work: Much of the work that exists on prostitution is not from those who work within the field, i.e., the prostitutes. As Nagle posits:

> ...theorizing is usually done by non-prostitutes (see, for example, Pateman, 1988). To momentarily don Marxist headgear, one could argue that the production of feminist discourse around prostitution by non-prostitutes alienates the laborer herself from the process of her own representation. While this is not to automatically discredit non-sex

worker feminist arguments against sex work, it is to say it is high time to stop
excluding the perspectives of sex worker feminists, time to stop assuming that
traditional feminist analysis of sexual oppression alone exhausts all possible
interpretations of commercial sex, and time to stop reproducing the whore stigma to
the larger culture. (Nagle, 1997, p. 2)

Not until recently has scholarship emerged from the workers themselves,
and much of what they are saying echoes the sentiments of the liberal
feminists. They take the position that prostitutes are in control of their own
bodies and are empowered in that they can make a decision to charge men for
what they are used to receiving for free. According to these groups, prostitutes
have made a conscious decision to enter the industry and they are aware of
other work options; they simply find sex work to be the most lucrative: "Most
women who work as prostitutes have made a conscious decision to do so,
having looked at a number of work alternatives" (Jenness, 1993, p. 406).

Rather than viewing themselves as exploited or without any other viable
economic opportunities, sex workers appeal to a "false consciousness" as they
see themselves as empowered and seek not to remove themselves from the
industry, but rather to legitimize their profession and to improve their
working conditions. In fact, groups such as COYOTE and HIRE have lobbied
on behalf of prostitutes for rights such as legalization of prostitution and
police protection. To sum up their position on sex work using their own
words, "[They] 'demand recognition as workers' and 'freedom to financial
autonomy...occupational choice...sexual self-determination...[and] worker's
rights and protections'" (Pheterson, 1989, p. 192–197).

Issues stemming from "mainstream" feminism: Mainstream feminism gained its
greatest momentum in the 1960s and 70s with a focus on confronting the
oppressions by all men of women. Since sexist behavior and oppression by
men is the central issue, mainstream feminism is often criticized as not
representing the issues of all women since Black women and other women of
color see racism as a primary concern (Omolade, 1994; Collins, 1990; Garcia;
1994; Ngan-Ling Chow; 1994; Lorde, 1984; hooks, 1981, 1984; Joseph &
Lewis, 1981). Since the mainstream movement has not always addressed
racism, and White women have not always acknowledged the privilege that

they enjoy from being White, the movement or perspective is considered mainstream because it marginalized women of color. However, more White feminists are now addressing issues of race and class (Palmer, 1994; Steinem, 1992; Lather, 1991).

Feminist perspectives of women of color: Many feminists of color have their roots in Marxism due to the fact that they see the oppression of people of color (both male and female) as a primary concern (Walker, 1983). However, the sexism that women of color face, even from males within their own race or ethnicity, is also central. It is for this reason that many women of color do not consider mainstream feminist perspectives to be representative or responsive to their needs and concerns. They therefore form their own perspectives. Though Black feminism was the first feminism stemming from women of color, many more feminists of color have developed theories specific to their own ethnic experiences such as Chicana, Asian, British, Puerto Rican, and so on.

Black feminist thought: Black feminism thought emerges out of the exclusion of the concerns and voices of African American women from the mainstream feminism movement and Black radical movements such as the Marcus Garvey and Black Panther movements (where women were an integral part but stood in the shadows of males who were considered to be the leaders), which probably can be more accurately identified as the White feminist movement. Even though the mainstream movement used an African American woman as its poster child, Sojourner Truth, it found no room for the voices of Black women. As a result, Black feminists began to speak to the needs and plights of African American women. According to much of Black feminist thought, Black women are uniquely oppressed because they are racially, socially, economically, politically, and sexually oppressed by this patriarchal society and White people (both men and women) as well as by Black men (Collins, 1990). Thus, the goal of Black feminism is to liberate Black women from all of these forms of oppression through social action (Combahee River Collective, 1986).

Due to the fact that Black feminists have been addressing issues of class for decades, and that I view prostitution largely as an issue of class, the perspective I employ is womanism as it is birthed out of Black feminist thought; yet it is inclusive of women of all races and ethnicities as well as men. Alice Walker defines womanism as:

> Womanist: A black feminist or feminist of color....A woman who loves other women, sexually and/or nonsexually. Appreciates and prefers women's culture, women's emotional flexibility...and women's strength. Sometimes loves individual men, sexually and/or nonsexually. Committed to survival and wholeness of entire people, male and female.[12] (Walker, 1982, p. xi)

In her anthology of womanist prose, *In Search of Our Mothers' Gardens*, Walker creates a more expansive definition of Black feminism by creating womanism, which is more inclusive than Black feminism. In Collins' essay, "What's in a name? Womanism, Black Feminism and Beyond," she compares womanism to feminism and finds that it is more encompassing for three reasons: (1) it is not anti-Black men and offers a means for African American women to address gender oppression without attacking African American men, (2) it is against all types of oppression and is committed to social justice, and (3) it does not limit its definition only to African American people but expands it all people of color[13]; as Walker writes, "'Mama, why are we brown, pink, and yellow, and our cousins are white, beige, and black?' 'Well you know the colored race is just like a flower garden, with ever color flower represented'" (1983, p.xi). Thus, womanism's purpose is primarily liberation from all types of oppression for African American women, but is not exclusive of men or other people of color. Due to the fact that womanism expands the definition of Black feminism in these key ways, many African American women choose to be defined as womanist. This contribution to the field of Black feminism by Walker is paramount.

Although womanist theory does not specifically address the issues of prostitution, it does address issues of sexual exploitation of women of all colors, sexual stereotypes of minority women, and social issues of race and class that are unique to minority women. It can be inclusive of all oppressed people and addresses the issue of marginalized women in general—even those of varied races and ethnicities who suffer from the same or similar social injustices as Black women. However, race and class also permeate the world of the prostitute. Therefore, while womanist theory is used since it is inclusive of all people who are oppressed, I also visited theories of race as was necessary for the analysis of data collected from the participants, all of whom were African American.

Black feminist thought addresses issues of sexual exploitation of women of color, sexual stereotypes of African American women, and social issues of race and class that are unique to women of color, but especially Black women due to the legacy of slavery. However, it fails to address prostitution on a broad scale:

> Perhaps the most curious omission has been the virtual silence of the Black feminist community concerning the participation of far too many Black women in prostitution. Ironically, while the image of African-American women as prostitutes has been aggressively challenged, the reality of African-American women who work as prostitutes remains unexplored....Examining the links between sexuality and power in a system of interlocking race, gender, and class oppression should reveal how important controlling Black women's sexuality has been to the effective operation of domination overall. (Collins, 1990, p. 164)

Collins feels that it is vital to explore prostitution as it relates to Black women, because for her it is at the nucleus of the race, class, and gender debate:

> The creation of Jezebel, the image of the sexually denigrated Black woman, has been vital in sustaining a system of interlocking race, gender, and class oppression. Exploring how the image of the African-American woman as prostitute has been used by each system of oppression illustrates how sexuality links the three systems. But Black women's treatment also demonstrates how manipulating sexuality has been essential to the political economy of domination within each system and across all three. (Collins, 1990, p. 174)

A Black prostitute echoes this position as she states:

> Speaking of Black women, I'd like to talk about the feminists....I cannot believe how many women were so biased against prostitutes. I heard, "How dare you think that you're a feminist. You're a prostitute. How can you do both of them?" And it's like, "How can I not?" I am a Black woman. I have always been the head of my family. I am the oldest of all the kids in my family. I take care of everybody. I am a feminist.

When I walk through the door you do not see a prostitute. You see a Black woman. (Nagle, 1997, p. 200)

For this Black prostitute, race, class, and gender are inseparable as she identifies all four realities in tandem in her statement. She is a prostitute, but she harkens to the reality that she is a Black woman (and the social oppression that that brings) and that her experience as such makes it necessary that she be a feminist. She refers to class when she states that she "takes care of everybody," even from her role as a sister. This is a role that many Black feminist theorists describe when they refer to the Black woman as caretaker or caregiver, i.e., the perpetual nanny (Collins, 1990; hooks, 1981). Thus, the Black woman, especially the prostitute, constantly lives at the intersection of race, class, and gender.

For those who do address prostitution, such as Collins and hooks, the sexuality of the Black prostitute is linked to the historical exploitation of Black women. Since Black women were exploited as slaves and raped by slave masters, society began to place slave women in the role of the prostitute, thus casting Black women as sexually promiscuous and willing to give sexual favors. "Since woman was designated as the originator of sexual sin, black women were naturally seen as the embodiment of female evils and sexual lust. They were labeled jezebels and sexual temptresses and accused of leading white men away from spiritual purity into sin" (hooks, 1981, p.33). However, this view of Black women left out a very critical component; Black women were not willing participants of their relations with White men, and for there to be an act of prostitution or "jezebelism" there had to be an exchange of money:

> Frequently, they used the term "prostitution" to refer to the buying and selling of black women for sexually exploitative purposes. Since prostitutes are women and men who engage in sexual behavior for money or pay of some kind, it is a term inaccurately used when applied to enslaved black women who rarely received compensation for the use of their bodies as sexual latrines. (hooks, 1981, p. 33)

In the case of Black slave women, there was no compensation for sex, as they were considered to be the property of the slave master; thus, any sexual activity was thought to be her duty and his right.

Another issue addressed by Black feminism is racial inequality between Black women and White women. Black females have fewer opportunities for traditional work, on account of the racial discrimination and inequality that Blacks face in general, such as less access to quality education. Therefore, more Black women than White women are forced to consider prostitution as an economic option. Also, when comparing White prostitutes with Black prostitutes, even within the industry, racial inequality persists as Black prostitutes are arrested at a disproportionate rate (McClintock, 1992; Bell, 1987; Alexander 1987). Thus, Black women suffer from the historical image as the "slave/whore" and face racial discrimination in the legal pursuit of prostitutes.

Conclusion of feminist theories and prostitution: Feminist theories on prostitution vary, from the position that it is degrading and sexually exploitative of women, and therefore depicting the prostitute as a victim, to the position that prostitution is a valid choice for women and that it is empowering for them to decide to do want they want with their bodies, depicting them as social agents of desire. However, the latter position does not take into account the fact that many prostitutes enter the industry when they are adolescents, and are thus relatively incapable to make an informed decision about prostitution. Also, it does not consider the fact that many women involved in prostitution have social and psychological histories that predispose them to such a lifestyle. Therefore, theories on prostitution that view prostitution as a cognizant and empowering choice by women should be expanded to address these facts.

Although feminist perspectives on prostitution exist, the larger feminist movement, which claims to be aimed at social equality for women, has not adequately addressed the issue of prostitutes, who suffer sexual, social, and economic oppression to great extent. This leaves prostitutes and sex workers with a feeling of not belonging and marginalization. As Laura Bell states:

> ... it is the definition of feminism that must change in order to include both good girls and bad girls, not they who must conform to a good-girl image so as to be considered feminist. Sex trade workers claim, in effect, to be feminists in exile, excluded from a rightful place in the feminist movement, they demand to be

recognized as members of the women's community. As one prostitute remarked, "Feminism is incomplete without us." (Bell, 1987, p.17)

CHAPTER THREE

Curriculum Theory and Dropping Out: The Nonschool Curriculum

In the previous chapters, female dropout theory and feminist theories of prostitution were examined. As I stated earlier in the female dropout theory chapter, the influences that affect girls' decisions to drop out were divided into push out and pull out factors. Again, push out factors refer to those influences in the school environment itself that push or force girls out of the school system. Those factors are interactions with teachers, classmates, administration, the curriculum, and extracurricular activities. Therefore, push out factors are related to the in-school curriculum. Pull out factors refer to what is known as the nonschool or out-of-school curriculum. It refers to interactions with the community, home, peers, media, and other influences outside of the school. For girls, the pull out factors tend to be related to their role as caretakers in their home environment, since many state that they leave to assist in taking care of ailing parents, siblings, or to get jobs to assist financially in the household. Since pull out factors are a major influence in the decision to drop out, the nonschool curriculum needs to be explored.

In Western society, the popular notion of what it means to be "educated" is largely defined by how much institutional schooling one has had (unfortunately, this view holds true among some educators as well). Thus, education, for the most part, is equated with this type of schooling. This narrowing of the concept of education is unfortunate, as education and knowledge are gained from many arenas, most of which are outside of the classroom. Knowledge not only comes from reading books, but through interacting with the physical world and applying that knowledge gained through schooling. The level or degree of schooling does not in and of itself make one knowledgeable; some of the wisest people may not have been formally schooled. Yet, they possess knowledge and wisdom that can never be adequately represented by a degree. Thus, much invaluable knowledge comes through nonschool curricula[14]; which I have come to regard as the treasures of what Gonzalez (1993) terms the "funds of knowledge". In Gonzalez's study, teams of teachers went to the homes of students and conducted research using an ethnographic design. They reported their findings to university faculty in an effort to find a way of bringing this wealth of information from the students' home environment into the classrooms. By incorporating the students' home experiences into their classroom curriculum, students were more engaged in learning, and a stronger relationship was established between the teachers, parents, and students

Many educators would agree that we learn from nonschool curricula; however, these curricula are largely neglected in research and in the compilation of in-school curricula. However, some educators and curricular theorists have long seen the value in nonschool curricula and have viewed it as an integral component to schooling. For example, almost 100 years ago Dewey wrote:

> Some kinds of participation in the life of those with whom the individual is connected are inevitable; with respect to them, the social environment exercises an educative or formative influence unconsciously and apart from any set purposes....it furnishes the basic nurture in even the most insistently schooled youth. In accord with the interests and occupations of the group, certain things become objects of high esteem; others of aversion....The main texture of disposition is formed, independently of schooling, by such influences. What conscious, deliberate teaching can do is at most free the capacities thus formed for fuller exercise, to purge them of some of their grossness, and to furnish objects which make their activity more productive of meaning. (Dewey, 1916, pp. 16–17)

Here, Dewey views the nonschool curricular influences of the social environment as the primary form of education, and the in-school curricula as only an enhancement to or providing direction for that knowledge.

Carter G. Woodson, also writing in the earlier half of the century, stated that students should be taught in a manner that reflects their natural environment; in other words, their nonschool curriculum should be used to teach concepts within school. In speaking of the successes of an American insurance man who succeeded in teaching Filipino children where trained teachers failed, he wrote:

> He had never taught at all, and he had never studied authorities like Bagley, Judd, and Thorndike; but he understood people. Seeing that others had failed, he went into the work himself. He filled the schoolroom with thousands of objects from the pupil's environment. In the beginning he did not use books very much, because those supplied were not adapted to the needs of the children. He talked about the objects around them. Everything was presented objectively....In teaching the Filipinos music he did not sing "Come shake the Apple-Tree." They had never seen such an object. He taught them to "Come shake the Lomboy Tree," something which they had actually done. (Woodson, 1933, p. 153)

Thus in the United States, the concept of using nonschool curricula in school is not new. It is more or less a return to the old. Some educators advocated the use of the nonschool curriculum in teaching at the beginning of the century; however, there was a drifting away from this stance. Soon, curricula that were taught in schools were pushed towards standardization, and the means of measuring the goals of curricula and the manner in which they were being implemented came to the forefront. Through this focus on the standardization and measurement of curricula, nonschool curricula began to be less important or ignored.

In the mid-1950s, the voices of dissension rose against in-school curricula that neglected or negated students' out-of-school experiences or curricula. These voices grew out of the civil rights movement. There was a movement back to the consideration of the nonschool curriculum due to the integration of schools, as students of color were marginalized and devalued in schools that taught them to be ashamed of their culture and daily lives (either through degrading cultures of color overtly or through glorifying White culture). Black curricularists called on the resurrection of theorists such as DuBois and Woodson, who called for a curriculum that reflected students' lives outside of school. While this might not have been expanded to the curricula learned from peers, it certainly focused on what was learned in the home and community.

Now we come to a modern or present-day movement that emphasizes making the nonschool curriculum more valuable by integrating and considering what students learn from their home, community, and among their peers. This raises an interesting question, one that Dewey addressed almost a century ago: Should the real life experiences of students, i.e., the nonschool curriculum, enhance the in-school curriculum, or should the in-school curriculum enhance the nonschool curriculum? While Dewey thought that the in-school curriculum should enhance the nonschool curriculum, this question is still of great debate.

Inherent in the in-school and nonschool curriculum debate is a false division of knowledge. The goal of curricularists today is to close this gap so that learning becomes holistic and that knowledge (both in-school and nonschool) becomes continuous, producing a well-rounded person who is better able to understand the world as a connected process. As Schubert writes:

> Life itself teaches the art of using knowledge. Life continuously enables reconstruction of our experiential maps of the world, our conceptions of how it works, where we fit in it, how we interact with it, and what is most worthwhile to do. Clearly, the development of such understanding is never fully made and always in the making. It is a lifelong process that involves all dimensions of living, including schooling. (Schubert, 1981, p. 186)

Thus, the guiding rationale behind curriculum is educating the holistic child for life.

Curricular theorists and educators who advocate for considering and using nonschool curricula in the creation of in-school curricula all seem to take a holistic approach to education. This means that knowledge should be continuous and should be able to be applied throughout all spheres of one's life. However, their rationales for using nonschool curricula vary. To say that there is variation among rationales is not to say that they conflict; it is simply to say that theorists travel different paths to get to the same point: that we must educate the whole child. The three rationales that I will consider are: cultural, student alienation, and social justice.

The Cultural Rationale

Curriculum is created with the goals of society in mind and rarely are the voices or life experiences of the students heard, although they are expressing their disconnection and discontent with their learning experiences (Ladson-Billings, 1994; Michie, 1999). This leaves the harsh reality that much of the curriculum that is developed and passed on to schools is created in isolation and without regard to the voices, sentiments, and life experiences of those most affected by it, the students (Freire, 1998). Thus, their experiences at home, in their community, and among peers are neglected or negated. This sends the message that the nonschool curriculum is not important, though nothing is further from the truth considering 18 hours of their day is spent outside of school.

The absence of students' voices and nonschool experiences is an issue for students of all races and ethnicities; however, students of color from various cultural backgrounds are especially marginalized because their lived experiences are not among those that are represented in the text that they encounter on a daily basis. In fact, much of what is termed education today can be more rightfully called assimilation, as students of color face cultural issues as fundamental as language differences in school on a daily basis. Thus, assimilation results in an educational experience that teaches, sometimes overtly, that the cultures of people of color are inferior and need to be replaced by Eurocentric models (Asante, 1987; Ogbu, 1978; Evans, 1988).

It is clear that the American schooling experience is aimed at establishing certain ideals and values in the minds of students, and that curriculum is a means to that end. As Boykin states:

> In the American public education system, schooling is more than the confluence of reading, writing, and arithmetic, so to speak. Indeed while these activities are going on, the schooling process also conveys certain ways of viewing the world, ways of codifying reality....It offers blueprints for living and for acceptable ways of functioning....It determines what is to be valued and esteemed and what are the proper forms of deportment and conduct. In short, there is a profound socialization agenda in schools, a cultural socialization agenda (Boykin, 1994; Hilliard, 1995; Banks & Banks, 1995). Thus, schools are not about reading, writing, and arithmetic per se. They are about the business of conveying such activities as they relate to certain cultural vantage points and as they are embedded in particular cultural substrates. Public schools were never conceived to be a culturally neutral exercise. (Boykin, 2001, p. 192)

However, these ideals and values do not align themselves with those of people of color; the curriculum excludes or marginalizes them, sometimes leaving students torn between the values of their culture and those Eurocentric values presented in school. Everyday, students are faced with the competing curricula of their culture and school.

In a study of student teachers, Liston and Zeichner showed that many prospective teachers come into the classroom after being taught a university curriculum that devalues people of color, and openly voice their desires for students to leave their culture behind and assimilate. As one student teacher states:

> ...Estella needs to change. Her parents need to let her go. She needs to leave her past and culture behind in order to succeed....Estella's life will be wasted if she ends up like her parents....Estella needs to assimilate to the predominant values of American culture. Estella and her family live in the United States and it they are going to thrive here, they need to recognize the values and structures of this society. (Liston & Zeichner, 1996, pp. 10–11)

Thus, students of color sometimes experience a curriculum where their culture is absent or devalued and that is further perpetuated by teachers who have not been taught to value other cultures. How do these realities affect these students' perceptions of themselves and the world around them?

The Student Alienation Rationale

When nonschool curricula are relegated to life outside of school and are not considered at all in the classroom, students begin to view their lives as students and their lives as children in their natural environment as dichotomous. They begin to feel that they need to make a choice between the two. Consequently, what is learned in school may not be that important, as it does not reflect anything else in their lives. Thus, they become disconnected from school and begin to feel alienated from their schooling experience. They begin to look for a level of comfort and a place of belonging, which could be from peers who are involved in destructive behaviors. In the case of the young women I studied, one of those places could be in their life of prostitution.

Although students are taught formally in school, the majority of their education takes place outside of school (Schubert, 1986), during the other 18 hours of the day. Everything they learn outside of school is not necessarily positive; nevertheless, it is familiar to them. If these things are not even considered in the classroom, whether it is to validate or disavow them, students could begin to feel that school is an isolated and fossilized experience. Thus, to minimize these feelings of disconnectedness, the way in which students live outside of school has to be examined. Many researchers have begun to do this in an effort to lessen alienation. For example, the Gonzalez (1993) study cited earlier shows how students' experiences in their home environment can enhance their in-school learning experience.

Gaining and utilizing knowledge learned from the nonschool curricula of students enhances their learning experience and makes them feel less alienated from the in-school curriculum; it also helps teachers feel less alienated from the students. Thus, it is important to create an environment where the learning process is mutual among the students and the teachers.

According to Lisa Delpit (1995), as summarized by Clardy et al. (2001), educators need to be students as well as teachers:

> 1. Educators need to know about their students' lives outside of school to determine social context and know the students' strengths that are perhaps hidden in school activities.
> 2. A problem that educators who are not from the community in which they teach face is the problem of ignorance of community norms. This ignorance fosters the formation of mistaken images/perceptions of parents and students.
> 3. We have created institutions of isolation, we need to connect the school with the home and the community. (Clardy et al. 2001, p. 10)

Thus, teachers and curricularists need to address the nonschool curriculum and understand how the failure to do so results in students who are alienated from their learning experience. Maybe when this gap between the two curricula begins to be actively addressed, the gap between teaching and the retention of knowledge will lessen.

The Social Justice Rationale

Many of the issues of discrimination and inequality go unaddressed in the classroom. Issues of racism, sexism, and classicism are ever present in our society, yet the discussion of these issues (or critical discussion of these issues) tends not to enter school for the most part. They are treated as though they are left at the doors of the school, when in fact they are present in the classrooms. Thus, these social justice issues are treated as nonschool curricula, meaning that they learn about these issues in their home and community, from peers, from the media, and elsewhere, or they are treated as "null" curricula, meaning that which is not taught in school (Eisner, 1979). Many educators and curricularists are advocating for addressing these social issues that students face on a daily basis within the curriculum and within the classroom in hopes of changing these things, hence "teaching for social justice". For example, in the earlier part of the century Black theorists such as DuBois and Woodson wrote about how racism was enacted in the school curriculum, and how Blacks were dissuaded from addressing political or social justice issues:

These Negro critics were especially hard on Negroes of our day who engage in agitation for actual democracy. Negroes themselves in certain parts join with the whites, then, in keeping out of the schools teachers [and hence, curriculum] who may be bold enough to teach the truth as it is. They usually say the races here are getting along amicably now, and we do not want these peaceful relations disturbed by the teaching of new political thought. What they mean to say with respect to the peaceful relation of the races, then, is that the Negroes have been terrorized to the extent that they are afraid even to discuss political matters publicly. There must be no exposition of the principles of government in the schools, and this must not be done in public among Negroes with a view to stimulating political activity. (Woodson, 1933, p.87)

Thus, the racism and political change that are taking place in society are ignored in school. Black theorists of today such as Banks and Banks (1998), Hilliard (2001), Boykin (2001), and Watkins (2001) agree that issues of social and political injustice are largely ignored in school curricula; however, racism is still largely relegated to the nonschool curriculum, meaning it is treated as something that only takes place outside of school.

In this age of technology, media have become an integral part of students' nonschool curriculum. It seems as though students spend more time on the internet, watching television, or listening to the radio than anything else. However, critical media literacy is rarely discussed in the in-school curriculum, though it has a strong impact on the way in which children view themselves and the larger world. For example, the way in which women are depicted in the media as sexual objects has a serious impact on the image that female youth form of themselves. It teaches them that women are valued according to their sexuality and physical beauty. Furthermore, when the in-school curriculum reinforces the status of women as inferior to men by creating curricula which largely exclude women, the stereotypical role of women is reinforced.

In this study, I explored the nonschool as well as the in-school curricula of female dropouts who are prostitutes, through unstructured interviews. What were their home, community, and peer interactions like? What were they taught in these environments? How did what they learn in school differ from what they learned out of school? What eventually made them choose their nonschool life over their in-school life? How do they view education and what was their schooling experience like? What are their views of women in this society? Where did they get those views? How were they treated as females in school and elsewhere? While research has been done on how girls are treated in school and on the inequity that they face (Henry, 1998; Horgan, 1995; McCormick, 1994; Fordham, 1993; WEEAP, 1990; Earle & Roach, 1989) research has not been conducted on these particular girls and their in-school and nonschool experiences. Because prostitution is laced with issues of gender, economic, and sexual oppression (prostitutes are arrested far more than their clients), the rationale that was used was one of the nonschool curriculum as a social justice issue.

Part Two

In Their Own Words

CHAPTER FOUR

"Nobody Cares": A Perspective from the Front Line

Stephen Cole

In America, we like to be spoon-fed our madness, not too much at once, and we don't want the lights too bright. We want the madness in a neat package. We need to be able to press a button and lower its volume, or punch another and remove it from view instantly. Don't serve it to us in its natural container, bulging chaos, incongruity and violence from every seam. We need it neat.

While we acknowledge that being a prostitute is a bad deal, we still want to package it in a pretty woman to numb the sting. We can do without the tales of beatings, robberies, rapes, and murder, thank-you-very-much. But if we dare to raise the covers high enough to peek underneath into the darkness that lurks beneath, what we find will rock even the most jaded of cynics. After a decade of being a street cop, I believe I can play the part of jaded cynic; if you can play the part of peeker, we make be able to take a good look, so let's ride.

The night felt as if it were made of ice. I remember this chill almost as much as I remember the seizing sight that grasped my heart when I saw this half-nude girl standing in front of the adult video store. High heels and a waist-length coat. Everything else from the waist down was nude. I pulled my squad car into the parking lot. Disbelief, the order of the night.

The clients of the adult video store moved in and out of the business' front door, barely casting a glance at the girl. I pulled my squad car in front of the store, and the girl approaches before I summon her. Just a normal part of her daily routine, police cars. As she draws near, I can see her youthfulness. She really is a girl. She still looks normal. Normal. A word I have adopted trying to yield order to the world of the prostitute. She looks like the girl next door, or the girl that sat behind you in math class, which is a big thing in this jungle. Jungle. Another adopted word. Before you know it, you've got your own language. The words are English but the meanings are different. Back to normal. This girl is still whole. I've seen 25-year-olds that look 60—scary, glossy 60 to boot. I've seen girls out here in the streets that look like movie stars, only to see them a year later and 200 pounds over the last weigh-in. Sad. But as this girl reaches the squad, I see she's normal and there's hope in that. Then she begins to tell her story, same as they all do, and normal seems like a pipe dream.

But first, I ask her name and birth date. Then the stock question I ask them all, "What are you doing out here?" The question is as silly as asking an astronaut where outer space is. But in this business, assumptions are bad. Better to hear the facts from their own mouths. She gives me a stock answer, mumbles something about making some money, and the ice is broken. Now we can take the gloves off. She senses I'm not about to read her the riot act and take my handcuffs out. So she's a little more comfortable talking to me. She tells me she is from a small Texas town, but she's street smart. She tells me she used to be overweight, but now the years have carved her into a woman. It's obvious her self-esteem is gone as she recounts the string of events that brought her to the streets. She dropped out of high school because of teasing over her weight and poor grades. She then left home to escape a sexually abusive stepfather.

Her voice falters and she looks past me, as she speaks of a party she attended at which she met three guys that gave her drugs, took her back to their apartment, and then took turns having sex with her. After finishing, they admonished her for being a whore and beat her before locking her in a closet. After freeing her from the closet two days later, they told her they were taking her to the street where she belonged, that way she could at least make them some money. A year into the ride, she learned the three guys were pimps all along and had used a technique they often employed to turn girls out. She tells me she doesn't have a pimp now and that she has been working the streets for four years.

After giving the girls the standard speech about the dangers of their occupations, the random and planned violence that lurks in the streets, they would volley the line right back to me. "You could get killed out here too. You could pull a car over, and bang."

That's right, I would tell them, but there would be honor in my death. I tell them I would be trying to do the right thing when death took me. In the Line of Duty and all that. No dice. I tell them I could meet God without having to avert my eyes, but they are unmoved. So I attacked them from the flank, seeing that the high ground yielded no results. Serial killers. The topic commands respect in any circle, and as the years would teach me, even more so among prostitutes. You can see it in their eyes. The uninterested glare is gone. No quick quips of the tongue. The first few times I discussed the subject with the girls, the fear I unmistakably recognized was born from the mythical status that the media had bestowed unto these madmen, whose names were like name brands: John Gacy, Ted Bundy, Jeffrey Dahmer, the Zodiac Killer, the Hillside Strangler, the Green River Killer. But after many conversations with these girls, it became clear to me that many of them had been in the presence of serial killers, these supercriminals that walk among us.

Many of the girls tell their stories of narrow escapes and lucky interventions by police officers "running a trick off" but only after the girls had seen the bottomless pits of these madmen's eyes. The thought gives me a chill. I don't remember a lot of the instruction given at the police academy. It's just not adaptable to the street. But one of the instructors gave a horrifying statistic. He stated that the Federal Bureau of Investigation estimated that there were 300 unknown serial killers operating in the United States at any given time. It seems those name brands only apply to the ones that slip up and get caught. I still can't get my mind around the 300. But it pales compared to the unsolved murders and Jane Does in county morgues across the country.

The normal-looking girl is looking at me now. She says she's freezing. Who am I to keep her in the cold? I ask myself. I tell the girl to go inside and find the rest of her clothing. I remind her that if she returns to her soliciting post, the next officer that comes by may very well use a much harsher tact. She turns and runs for the door of the video store and I pull from the stop and head for the exit, and the waiting streets, sure that the night was young and the worst hiding behind the dark horizon.

There is great diversity to the depths of dissipation in the streets. Every race is accounted for. The common thread is economic disadvantage, but even this doesn't always hold true. I've seen the daughter of a Russian immigrant scientist and a third generation 16-year-old prostitute that was the daughter of a legendary pimp. Both in the world of prostitution for reasons that were worlds apart.

The majority of the girls are younger than 19 and have very little in the way of education and job training. The sex industry appears to be a simple way to self-sufficiency and fast money.

Once immersed into the fast and cruel existence of the prostitute, the girls soon realize that the same racism and classicism exists in the sub-culture of the prostitute. Johns and tricks often prefer White females to Black females, and the young before the old, and the prices they are willing to pay will reflect this desire. The duality that surrounds the pricing of sex for sale puts many of the Black girls in a situation that causes them to perform twice the work of a girl in a more preferable race or ethnicity, and this element of the prostitute's work life makes them a double victim.

The desire for money drives the business of prostitution. Many of the young girls encountered in the street view prostitution as the only opportunity afforded to them by society. Many feel locked out of the traditional income earning world. Most believe they can never overcome their lack of education and most continue the remainder of their lives in the underworld of sex for money. It is a sad state and an indictment against the "American dream".

Nobody likes a prostitute. This is the vicious catch-22 of the prostitute. Even the john or the trick that seeks her out and pays his money often wants to exact a sort of revenge or domination over the working girl. I've had girls explain how "dating" a trick was a lot like two rabid animals circling each other, looking for the perfect moment to pounce.

This type of duality often carries over into the way the average police officer talks and interacts with a prostitute. Officers have been known to call the girls "whores" and "bitches" and to treat them with disrespect and disdain usually reserved for cop-killers. After all, who would they complain to? Who in their right mind would believe such a mild verbiage would offend a prostitute? This type of behavior elevates the prostitute to a rare platform of perpetual victim because very few people are tormented by both the good guys and bad guys on a daily basis. It is the rare man indeed that hasn't had his heart broken by a woman, usually in the form of some sexual betrayal, and the prostitute often becomes the symbol of this past malign.

This very thought was weighing on my mind when my squad car entered the intersection and I saw a women dart in front of a red Chevy Suburban two cars in front of me, narrowly missing the front of the vehicle.

As the woman escaped certain injury and darted into the parking lot of the gas station, I noticed that one of the heels was broken off her shoe and one of the sleeves on her jacket was torn at the seam where the upper arm meets the shoulder. I pulled into the parking lot and turned on my overhead lights. I was in the lot two seconds before I noticed the woman's attire and made her for a prostitute. She had her fake waist-length fur coat open and a fishnet top that revealed her bare breast underneath. She had on a miniskirt that had obviously been altered to be even shorter; boots that came up above the knee and below the thigh completed the attire. Opening my door, I exited the squad car and headed towards her. Tears were streaming down her face and she was fumbling in her purse by the time I reached her.

I ask her, "What's the problem, why the mad dash into the traffic and how did you come by the torn jacket?"

She looked at me with watery eyes, and I could see swelling under her left eye. She told me that she got picked up by a guy about two blocks away from where we now stood and he took her to his apartment complex, which was just around the corner. Once they arrived, there was an argument on the previously negotiated price of $100. He now wanted to pay $50. When she refused, he back-handed her in the face. She opened the door to get out and he pulled a knife from under his seat, grabbing her by the arm. She pulled away, tearing her jacket in the process.

I ask her to get into my squad car with me and take me to the location. She refuses, tells me that the guy chased her out of the parking lot and probably hasn't returned, if he ever really lived there at all. I ask her if she wants me to make an offense report. She looks at me with a dead stone face and simply says, "Why? Nobody cares."

The words were so sharp and crisp on the freezing night, they sounded like a dark epithet for the entire human race. I gathered my response after a few seconds, taken aback by the complete certainty in her voice. I tell her that's not true. I tell her. I ask her about her family and she tells me her father was killed while serving time in prison for murder and that her mother, a former prostitute, is a heroin addict. She says the rest of her family back in Oklahoma doesn't want anything to do with her.

I ask her how old she is and find out that she's 23. Her phone rings. After a few minutes she says a few cryptic phrases. I know she's talking to her pimp. After she hangs up, I ask her about the pimp. She says she has been with him five years and he takes care of her. They live in a four bedroom house tucked away in a suburb. They have two Cadillacs and he takes her and her wife-in-law (prostitutes sharing the same pimp) shopping everyday. She says it's all the family she has now. I ask her if she wants me to call for an ambulance to have a look at her. She asks me why I'm being so nice to her. I tell her that first, I'm treating her they way I would treat want someone to treat my daughter or my sister, and that second, I'm trying to do my job. She says no to the ambulance, and tells me she's already lost time and money. Once again I try to convince her to report the assault and give me any information she can on the suspect and his vehicle. She gives me a vacant and lost smile, then says she's been raped at gunpoint five times, beaten and robbed at least seven, the last time the perpetrator thought she was dead and left her behind a convenience store unconscious with her dress pulled over her head. Another working girl found her and called 911.

The words didn't come to me so quick this time. I rebounded and told her to at least give me her name and her birthdate. While I was writing, she asked me why society was so screwed up. She said they paid ballplayers millions of dollars to do what they would probably do for free, if given the choice of playing ball or working a nine-to-five job. Then she said the same ballplayers come out to the streets and turned tricks with the same girls that society looked upon as throwaway people.

"They don't give the teachers nothing though," she said. "No wonder schools are churning out losers."

As I finished writing, she gave me an apologetic "thank you" and turned to continue on her way across the parking lot, when she stopped. She looked at me and said, "Don't spend too much time worrying about the guy. In a little while it will be like it never happened. I'll forget about it just like I do with everything else. I pretend nothing bad ever happened to me or anyone else, it helps me not to care."

I watched her for a good while as she crossed the lot and made her way across the street. The night stalking was all too much. Cops and killers, prostitutes and pimps.

I closed my black book full of names and birthdates, and watched as the woman disappeared into a wave of traffic, the faces of the motorists as uncaring as the falling moonlight.

I climbed into my squad car thinking that someone has to be able to get the word out. Shout it in a way in which it can be heard. Maybe find the root of the problem and ultimately, a solution.

As I pulled my squad car back into traffic, my optimism waned. My final though was that maybe she was right. In the final analysis, it could be a stark fact: nobody cares.

CHAPTER FIVE

Carmella's Story: "My Baby Didn't Have No Pampers and No Milk"

"I got a story to tell you," the young woman said whom I came to know as Carmella. After an introduction between her and I in which she interrogated me about who I was and what my purpose was, I was very surprised that she was interested in participating in the study. When I first told the women about the study, many replied that they had dropped out of school but had not been involved in prostitution. Because I had attended a conference on prostitution recently, I knew that many people involved in the industry defined it in different ways. Some call it "survival sex"; therefore, they do not consider it prostitution as they view that as a chosen activity. Survival sex means that the activity is necessary for their survival (shelter, food, etc.) and not a choice (Greene, 1999; Boyer 1993). Some had a problem with the term "prostitution" because it brought to mind someone standing on the corner to sell sex and did not include other forms of trading sex for money. Because of the various definitions of prostitution, the women and I decided to define it as trading sex for money, goods, shelter, food, or clothes—even if they are for the benefit of another (i.e., a child, sibling, parent, or other loved ones). Once it was defined in this way, many of the women agreed that they indeed had been involved or were currently involved in prostitution.

Carmella was one of the women who scowled when I mentioned prostitution. She went on to show her disdain by grilling me in front of the other women. "I ain't no prostitute and I got my G.E.D. four months ago," she said in a way to let me know this study wasn't for her. I must admit, I was intimidated by her. I definitely felt like an outsider, trying to peer into their lives. I distinctly remember sweat pouring down my back as I tried to maintain my cool, trying not to look as scared as I really was. So I emphasized that I wasn't insinuating anything, that I just wanted to introduce the study to them just in case some of them might qualify and be interested in participating. Again, I listed the qualifications: you must have dropped out of traditional school (meaning those with a G.E.D. could still participate), you must be at least 18 (though I didn't want women over 25), and you must have been involved in prostitution prior to 18 (and we adjusted the definition of prostitution as I described above). Still, she sat there, commanding the conversation.

Eventually other women spoke out, "I'm too old," "Honey, you don't want me," "I got an associate's degree." Those who didn't reply looked away in disinterest. Soon I told them that I would be in another room if any of them wanted to get more information about the study. I stood up from the table and the defensive air in the room was deflated as they looked at my seven-month pregnant belly. They immediately started to nurture me saying, "Oh, I didn't know you were pregnant, I couldn't tell while you were sitting down. Do you need some water, it's hot? Girl, go get her some water." I spent the next 15 minutes talking about my pregnancy and answering the usual questions, "Do you know what you're having? Is this your first one? Are you married?" They told me how proud they were of me that I was married and had gotten my education prior to having a baby. Many of them shared with me that they had children as well. I began not to feel all that different from these women, as I looked at their faces, brown like mine, and as I felt their palms on my belly. I felt a connection and my fear began to dissipate. Soon, they reconsidered and wanted to know how they could help me. Again, I told them that I would speak with them individually in the other room. I left the room feeling more confident and at ease. A few minutes later, Carmella appeared in the doorway and that was beginning of our journey together.

"I want you to tell me about your childhood, how you grew up, stuff like that. Tell me your story," and with that Carmella began to share the story she had promised, and what a story it turned out to be. She grew up on the west side of Chicago in an area infamous for its socioeconomic strife. Her community was one riddled with gangs and drugs, as she stated matter-of-factly when I asked her to describe the community in which she grew up.

"Gangs and drugs," she said. Yet she added that she felt comfortable in her community, "Because my grandmother, they had a house there. They raised us up there. It's been like 40 years. I liked my community, I knew everybody." However, though she felt comfortable and safe in her community, her feeling of safety came from the respect that her family gained due to their dealings in the "street life". She made it clear that she did not consider her neighborhood "safe", as she painted her vision of a neighborhood in which she would like to raise her son.

"No drugs, no coming out your house and soon as you step out your house somebody running by and selling drugs, the police chasing them, gang-related, I mean all sorts of ooooh, you know what I mean? When you send your child out the door you got to get on your knees praying that they make it back in safely. Bullets not coming in the window and you sitting on the couch and one gone come in and hit you in the back of your head."

She described her life as an only child in a household with extended family, "My grandparents, my grandmother and my granddad, aunts and uncles, my mother." Though her family was close-knit, her household was very busy because no one knew she was in the house when she ditched school. "By my grandmother house being as big as it was, everyone was occupied and they didn't know if I was in the house or not. It was a big house and I used to hide in the basement. So that was it, days and days and days were going by and I wasn't in school." Paradoxically, though there were many adults in the house, including her mother, no one supervised her closely, and that, coupled with the "street life" in which her family and community were steeped, allowed her the time and skills needed to indulge in mischief.

When Carmella was a young child, they were very poor, often times lacking basic necessities such as adequate clothing. This led to problems with other students at school. "I liked to be in school, it's just that I used to get picked on all the time... my mama, she worked. I didn't have many things. Sometime I had to wear the same clothes a whole month." However, this didn't remain to be the case because she describes her life as a teenager differently, "[I had] a car, clothes, money, jewelry. My mom and dad had plenty of money."

Though she had a difficult childhood, she still maintained that it was all right. I asked her, "Before high school would you say that you had a good life?"

She replied, "It was okay. It wasn't messed up like, but my mama made the best of it. Then my life, it just changed from good to worst, rags to riches."

Carmella loved education because she loved being taught new things; however, she did not like her schooling experience partly because of boredom and mostly because of the social issues she faced. She was in constant conflict with the girls in school. Many of those led to confrontations, which led to fights. She credited all of these problems to jealousy over the way she looked and the material things she had. "During grammar school, it was rough for me going to grammar school. Girls used to beat me up all the time. So I guess that was a part of jealousy." The bad relations with her female classmates followed her to high school, as she often talked about fights and arguments that occurred. As a result of what she described as jealousy, she never made friends within school. Instead, her cousins were her friends. Thus, she never had a social connection to school. When she became pregnant at 16, the decision to drop out was not difficult to make. So, in her junior year, she dropped out to have her son and met a man who moved her out of her grandmother's house and introduced her to prostitution. What followed was a life of prostitution, at first for survival, then for money—eventually, for a lavish lifestyle and to support a heroin and cocaine drug addiction. What follows is the story of Carmella's effort to connect the dots of her life and her current efforts to reclaim what she says is, "...the identity Satan took from me."

Dropping Out: "I Was Just Making Bad Decisions During That Time"

Don't Like Social Studies, Don't Like Science

On many occasions, Carmella told me that she always enjoyed the act of learning, "I liked to be in school, teach me something. Right today it's like teach me what I don't know. If I don't know it teach me. I'd be quiet and listen." However, though she was excited about learning, she had conditions on what she wanted to learn and from whom she would learn them. For example, she detested social studies and science. This was unfortunate because they happened to be the last two classes on her schedule for both her freshmen and sophomore years. She often cut those periods, leaving school early. In fact, she attended these classes so infrequently that she was hard-pressed to remember that they were the last two classes of the day when I asked her to recite her class schedule. Even today, she still didn't quite know why she disliked those classes.

"My eighth- and ninth-period classes, I never hardly went to. [They were] my last periods. A lot of times—I really didn't like her. I just didn't go. It was the whole day and we didn't get out 'til late....My eighth- and ninth-period classes was my freshmen year, social studies. I did not like social studies, didn't like that class, I just didn't like it. I never knew why. Social studies and science I didn't really like. I hated science. I didn't want to experience nothing. No cutting up no frogs; I have a weak stomach. Social studies was my freshmen year. My sophomore year, I think I had social studies again. That's one class I failed in, social studies."

A Teacher's 'Right' to Teach

Another factor that affected her willingness to learn was her opinion of the teachers' "right" to teach the subject. She related this to me as she described her experience in an American history class (focusing on Black slavery) taught by a White man.

"History. It never seems to fail. Why is there a White person teaching Black people history," she said.

"Did you ever have a Black history teacher?" I asked, hoping that she would be able to tell me how the two learning experiences were different.

"No never. So I always wanted to know why was this White person teaching Black people's history? And that used to just get away from me. How could you tell us something about our race? So I say, 'Let's do it like this. Let one of us teach and you get back there and you sit down. You have to read your books to find out. You not teaching us nothing.' He couldn't teach us nothing and that's the way I looked at it then."

"What did he say to that?" I asked, curious as to how that kind of confrontation was handled.

"Only thing I recall him saying is that he...he was a racist person anyway."

Since she didn't give a clear explanation, I probed further. "Why would you say that?"

"I just felt that he was racist 'cause when I come into history class...maybe he was just racist towards...maybe he just didn't like me. I'm gone take that back. Maybe he didn't just like me. 'Cause I'd come to his class and take over his class. Every single day 'til he just...they had to switch my class. I got kicked out of history. I just don't see why White people teaching history. They wasn't in slavery. That's the bottom line."

She never really gave an example of a specific problem that she had with the content of his teaching or his teaching style. She resented having the history of her people being taught by someone who wasn't a legacy of slavery.

Attitude

Though Carmella said that she would, "be quiet and listen" if someone was teaching her something, this was not always the case. She said that she often had "run-ins" with the teachers because of her poor attitude. Sometimes these confrontations with her teachers led to interruptions in class and a reputation for being a difficult student. When I asked her about her behavior in school, specifically prior to her dropping out, she described it as poor towards her teachers and other students.

"I just had an attitude. Just a snotty individual, an attitude."

"With other students and the teachers or just..." Before I could finish the question, she clarified it for me.

"Just period. Period."

"Did anyone at school notice your behavior? Know that you were acting just a little worse?" I asked, wondering if her attitude had become unmanageable.

"It wasn't so much as worse than an attitude," she said, meaning that she didn't act-out; she was just very unpleasant in the classroom.

"Did the teachers say something about it?"

"Yeah, I used to get a lot about my attitude, that's really what it was."

"So what did they do about it?"

"It was nothing they could do about it." It seemed not to occur to her that they could have sent her to the discipline office or had her expelled.

"Did they ever kick you out?" I asked, knowing that many teachers have students suspended for insubordination.

"Naw."

"So they just left you in the classroom?" I was surprised that the teachers would continue to deal with this inside the classroom since she said that she often had a bad attitude in class.

"Yeah."

"Ignored you or what did they do?"

"It was my mess I had to deal with it and that's what I was taught for a long time. 'It's your mess, you have to deal with it.'"

"So did you ever disrupt the class or anything like that? I asked, since as a teacher, I know that students with bad attitudes often have to be addressed during classroom time.

"Naw. Just don't bother me."

"Don't bother you and you were cool?" She didn't disrupt class as long as no one disturbed her in any way.

"Right."

Though she faced issues in class because of her self-described poor attitude, she was never officially disciplined by the school for it. "I ain't never get suspended. I have never been expelled from school, suspended from school. Never kicked out from school."

Rivalry with Female Schoolmates

Carmella was a loner in school. The only friends that she had were her cousins, one of whom attended the same high school. From the time that she was in grammar school, Carmella encountered conflict with female classmates. "...I used to get picked on all the time. My hair was real extremely long and they used to pull my hair all the time." This issue only intensified when she reached high school, as she described the conflicts that took place between her and girls as related to her looks, the fact the boys found her attractive, and the material things that she owned (a car, clothes, and jewelry).

"I dealt with a lot of jealousy, 'cause I got a lot of attention," Carmella told me.

"A lot of attention from boys in school?" I asked, thinking that that could be the kind of attention that might spurn jealousy among teenage girls.

"Yeah, too much," she answered.

"And so were they jealous about that?"

"That's where it came in. Then coming around to high school. As a freshie I had a car, a lot of girls didn't," she explained. I began to wonder how having a car affected her school attendance. I wanted to know how it affected her cutting school or classes. "So, you had a car? So did you go to school all the time?"

To my surprise she replied, "Uh-huh," indicating yes.

"You went everyday?" I had to clarify this because she told me earlier that she cut school quite often as she was nearing the time when she dropped out. I wondered if she cut school as often when she was a freshman.

"Everyday. That's why my momma and daddy bought it, just for me to go to school everyday." Again she insisted.

"Did you live far from school?"

"No I didn't, I could have walked. It was one bus to catch to school, straight shot. Like 10 minutes from the house."

"So you were the only kid so they got you a car?" I asked because I wondered why her parents would buy her a car as a freshmen since she lived so close to the school.

"Right."

"And they were jealous of that?" I asked, thinking that this was one of the sources of conflict between her and the girls.

"They were jealous about that 'cause I came. You know you ain't supposed to receive no car 'til your senior year."

"Right," I answered because from my experience when I was a student and as a teacher, it was unusual for a freshman to have a car.

"I had one the freshie year," she said in a tone of pride. Because the car added to her strained relationship with girls in school, I was curious about how the conflict affected her feelings about school. "Okay, well was there ever a time when you didn't like school?"

"Yeah," she answered as though that should have been obvious.

"Tell me what was going on at that time?" I asked, wanting her to elaborate on the social situation at school during that time.

"I was fighting a lot," she said emphasizing "a lot".

"And what were your fights usually about?"

"Jealousy," she answered.

"What kind of things were the girls jealous of?" I prompted for further explanation.

"The way I look, the way I carry myself...and I hung out with all the guys."

"So what in particular were they jealous about at that time?"

"Car, clothes, money, jewelry."

"And what about you would you say that guys liked a whole lot? What was attractive to the guys?"

"My personality, plus I had a shape." I found it interesting that she said that guys liked her personality in high school because she later described her relationship with men throughout her life as only wanting sex, only wanting her body.

What Girls Envy

From the first time that I talked with Carmella, 10 minutes into our conversation she told me that she had a difficult time in school with the other girls because she had "long, good hair." She described "good hair" as hair that has a soft, curly, wavy texture. It was not surprising to me that she experienced a lot of strife due to her hair because in the African American community, the length and texture of one's hair has historically been of great importance (Ansariyah-Grace, 1995; Grayson, 1995). "Nappy" hair or tightly coiled hair historically has been something to be ashamed of as African Americans have tried to assimilate into White culture; hence, the straightening processes such as press and curls and relaxers (better known as perms). It was strange to hear her talk about the long, finely textured hair she had while growing up because her hair was now damaged from years of chemical treatment. We talked further about what other things the girls were jealous of, focusing this time specifically on hair and physique.

"Did you have long hair? You brought that up earlier," I asked in an effort to expand on our earlier conversation.

"Really long hair," she answered.

"The reason I'm asking about that is because that tends to be a big issue in the Black community. I know when I was in school that was a big issue, if you had long hair." I told her about my own experience in school because I was aware of what she was talking about.

"Long hair, nice shape," she added. Since she had both of these attributes, which are highly coveted among African American girls, the potential for jealousy and conflict was great (Ansariyah-Grace, 1995; Grayson, 1995). "And so you had a lot of fights," I added. Carmella began to give examples of the particular issues that led to fights. "How old were you when you were having those fights?"

"I'm a freshman, but it started from grammar school."

"Okay, but it got to the point when it was over the top when you were a freshman? Did you like school when you were in elementary school?" I asked, curious if she experienced the same strife as a grammar-school student.

"No," she replied.

"Why not?"

"Fights."

It soon started to appear as though Carmella had been involved in fights with her peers throughout her schooling. "Okay, so when would you say you started having real problems with fighting in school?"

"Grammar school."

"Like at what grade?" I wanted to know if this started around the time that girls typically began to like boys and compete for their attention.

"Seventh."

"Seventh grade?" I wasn't surprised because 13- and 14-year-old girls are usually interested in boys.

"Right," she replied.

"What do you think started the problems?" I wanted to know if these were the same issues that started the fights in high school, namely jealousy.

"My hair," she answered. I had real long hair."

"Why do you think that was an issue, the fighting about the hair?" I wanted her to elaborate on why hair was such a big issue for the girls.

"Because they want to pull it all out," she said.

"Why do you think they want to pull it all out?" I continued to probe.

"So you won't have none," she added matter-of-factly.

"What I'm getting at is that White girls, I don't know if they really have this kind of problem with wanting to pull each other's hair out and fighting over hair. So what do you think is going on with that?" I asked, wanting to know if she had a deeper understanding as to why hair length and texture was so important to African American girls.

"You know what, that's a good question," she said slowly as she thought about it.

"Cause you know they don't fight like that about hair," I wasn't suggesting that they don't envy certain hair types, colors, and textures; only that to my knowledge they don't physically fight about hair lengths and plot to snatch each other's hair out over it.

"Right, 'cause you know 9 times out of 10, Black women hair is not long, they add hair to their hair. And my hair was long and my skin was clear and pretty and my mama kept me neat from head to toe, everything matched. All the boys liked that and I didn't have friends in grammar school 'cause everybody wanted to talk about me or fight me."

So having what all the other girls wanted, long, finely-textured hair, a nice shape, and clothes did not make her more popular as one might have expected. Instead, it made the other girls despise her enough to want to inflict physical harm on her. So, she had become a leper of sorts, because of her classmates' envy of her. She was the proverbial "girl everyone loved to hate" and her self-described "bad attitude" could not have helped.

"So what do you think was the greatest problem? Was it because you had things or because the way you look? What started the most problems?" I asked because being disliked for something external such as clothing could have a different emotional and psychological effect as it is something that can be changed. Being disliked for the way one physically looks is something much more personal because it is not as easily altered, especially for a teenager without the financial means to do so.

"The way I look," she answered.

Hair was a huge issue. Because I wanted to understand this concept, I asked her to describe her hair since it was the focal point of so many conflicts. "So did you have a perm at that time?"

"No, press and curl. I messed my own hair up by putting chemicals in it, stuff like that," she said as she pulled her fingers through her hair which was literally standing straight up on her head. By "messing up" her hair she meant that it had broken off because she was tugging at the ends of her hair. Now, her hair wasn't the long mane that was so envied by the girls. I could not see the texture of the hair she had as a young girl because it had been relaxed and was straight.

"Right, didn't we all?," I chimed in because I understood the dynamics of African American hair since I used to chemically straighten my hair and also had over-processed my hair with relaxing straighteners many times before.

"I had really good hair." She answered proudly.

The concept of "good hair" is familiar among African American people. It typically is defined as hair that is not hard or "nappy" or tightly curled.

Instead, it is wavy, softer, and/or straight. In essence, hair that appears to be similar to Caucasian hair. "Okay, so that was a problem too. Not only did you have real long hair, you had a 'nice' grade of hair."

"Yep," she clarified.

The Fights

For almost as long as Carmella could remember, she was involved in fights at school. Though I never directly asked her who started the fights, she was clear in telling me that she was always picked-on by girls at school. She definitely considered herself to be the victim. However, she never described any conflict with boys. Instead, the boys really liked her because of her personality and her looks, she told me. In fact, this was a constant source of friction between Carmella and the other girls. And though she admits that she had a bad attitude, she never saw that as a reason for the fights, only jealousy. So, by the time she reached high school, the social tension between Carmella and other female students had increased. "So as far as the social environment, would you say that was worse or better in high school?"

Carmella thought for a moment and replied, "It was worse 'cause these bunch of girls got they clique. When one roll, a lot of them roll. One jump on you, all of them jump on you."

This was horrible for Carmella since she didn't have a clique. As she stated earlier, she was a loner and the only friends she had were her cousins and only one of them attended her school. "What did the teachers say about that, the fights? Were you in the discipline office a whole lot?"

She let me know that she was a whole lot smarter than that, "I would never fight in school. They never fight on school grounds. They always want to fight when I'm leaving out 'cause wasn't nobody trying to get suspended and my freshie, my sophomore, and my junior year, I ain't never get suspended. I have never been expelled from school, suspended from school. Never kicked out from school."

"So when would the confrontation start?" I asked, since she was clear that there was no fighting in school.

"A block or two over," she answered.

I wanted to get more details about the fights, since she was constantly involved in them.

"I mean, but usually, somebody starts talking stuff in school, see what I'm saying?" I prompted because I wanted to find out if they would wait all day to settle scores.

"Right," she confirmed.

To describe how the fights started and how they were handled, she told me about an incident that led to a brutal fight—one in which she was attacked by a group of girls. It all started over "he said, she said" gossip.

"You know, I remember one time me and my boyfriend went to the same school and another chick wanted him and they came like, 'Such and such is trying to get up with your guy.' I said, 'He grown, he make his own decisions.' They went back and said that I said, 'If she don't leave my man alone, we gone fight.' I never said that. My car was parked, I never would park my car in front of the school, on the next block. I was on my way home and he had left two periods before I did and I'm on my way to my car. I was waiting on my cousin, but she went back to school for something and here they come, 'You said you wanna...' I ain't said nothing. There go the fight. She came with a lot of friends. They jumped on me. After they jumped on me, by that time my boyfriend came. My cousin got my car and we went back over there. By that time, her and all her friends on the porch. They said [the boyfriend and her cousin] 'Go on the porch,' and I went on the porch and I whupped her ass on the porch and into the house. I whooped her ass. They was always a bunch of punk bitches. They want to jump on people at one time. 'Fight her one-on-one and I bet you right now she'll whoop all y'all ass.' And they didn't want to do nothing. And when I came out of there, there was one more girl and I hit her so hard, I knocked her backwards. I came to school and everything with my black eye and everything, my scratches on my face. Soon I was right back all pretty and everything. I could walk down the halls and they wouldn't bother me because they knew I could fight.

Hustling

Carmella used the word hustling to describe illegal activities. She told me that she got to a point where the only reason that she was attending school was to make money from selling drugs. As she explained, "I wasn't in school to fight. I was in school hustling." Because this term is often used to describe various criminal activities such as drug dealing and prostitution, I asked her to clarify how she was using it at this point, "What do you mean by hustling?"

She told me, "Selling weed."

This was an activity that was common in her community and in which her family was involved. Once I was talking with her about her cousins, who were her only friends, and I asked her if they were involved in any criminal activities, to which she replied, "The whole family was involved." Though her family dealt in drugs, she was not introduced to selling by them. In fact, her son's father introduced it to her when he gave her a supply to sell at school.

"My baby daddy used to give me weed to sell. Everybody in school was getting high. He used to give me weed and stuff to take to school and sell."

Drug dealing was something that Carmella struggled with in high school and also today. Ironically, though Carmella has dealt in prostitution since she was 16, the times that she was arrested and spent time in jail were for selling drugs. At the time in which I was conducting interviews with her, she was awaiting a trial date for selling drugs. In fact, she had spent years on and off in jail for dealing. "Two years was the longest time and everything else off and on eight months, nine months. And that two years was for drugs."

The Schools' Services for Pregnant Girls

When Carmella left school, she was a junior and was 16 years old. Though she had plenty of conflict with girls in school and cut classes often, she told me that she liked going to school and learning new things. In fact, she rarely was absent from school for a whole day, only select classes like social studies and science. So I asked her why she left, to which she replied, "I was pregnant." She told me that she had a challenging pregnancy and left school during her fifth month, but admitted that the school was very accommodating to girls in that predicament.

"Did you feel like you had any support? Did anybody know you were pregnant, like the teacher?"

"Everybody."

"So was there anyone who talked with you about the options for staying in school?"

"Yes, I was just too big to stay in school. I was five months then."

"Okay. I think it's a little bit different in school now. Let's talk about what it was like being in school pregnant then, because I don't think you have to go to pregnant school now. I think you had to go to pregnant girl school then."

"No, at West High School they had everything there already. It was just a lot of teenagers who were pregnant. So, it was all in school, the day care, they provided it. The things you needed they provided you at that school. The doctors, prenatal care. You can go find out about your baby."

"Oh, they had doctors there?"

"Yeah. They had doctors at the high school. Yeah. They had a lot going on at that school. A lot of support there."

"Did they send you to a counselor or anyone to talk to when you were pregnant? Did you go to a counselor?" I asked.

"Yeah, I went to a counselor. They was acting really shocked, but I knew I was having sex, so hey. Yeah. I went to a counselor and I was like what I'm gone do?"

"So how did the counselor advise you? Was it a woman?"

"Yeah, she was a woman. Everything free that was out here, she told me to get it. She gave me a lot of referrals to get here and there."

"You said you were sick so you missed a lot of school so they had to put you on home schooling?" I asked, because from my teaching experience, students who are unable to attend school must be accommodated by a homebound teacher who teaches the student at home at least once per week when they are unable to physically attend school.

"Right."

"So did you have an opportunity to return to school to keep up with the home schooling?"

"Yeah. I had an opportunity to return to school." So the school was making efforts to retain her.

"Okay. So how long were you home schooled by the homebound teacher?"

"Uh, I left school at five months; I left in August. It was just beginning, that school year. I was just making bad decisions during that time."

"Okay, like what?"

"I'm gone leave pregnant. I could have went back to school and graduated."

"So the homebound teacher started. What did you do when she came?" I asked, wanting to know more about how she adjusted to a one-on-one teaching environment.

"I wasn't there. We got a couple of studies in. I was studying and after that I was always at the doctor. I had really got sick, I had gestational diabetes and I was at the doctor everyday, every single day. So that was interfering with my teacher coming out 'cause I'm always sick. Then, I was threatening a miscarriage. Every time you turned around, I was threatening a miscarriage. So that interfered with that. So keeping up was...understand? So, they had said just come back to school and then when I didn't show up they was coming out there. You know, come back to school, come back to school."

"So then the homebound teacher...you just kinda slid between the cracks?"

"Yeah."

"They stopped calling and everything?"

"Yeah. They checked back in, but I was like I'm putting that on hold. I'm coming back."

"You were working at that time? Where were you working?" I reminded her of what she told me earlier.

"McDonald's." Caremella told me that she had worked for McDonald's on a few occasions over the years.

"Okay. And you worked full time?"

"Uh-huh." Since she worked full time, it was difficult for her to commit to school. Her priorities had been rearranged.

Attendance

For the most part, Carmella had pretty consistent attendance during her first years of high school. She rarely described missing a full day of school. However, there were classes that she hardly attended like social studies and science. When she reached the middle of her sophomore year, she began to cut school a lot, missing entire days.

"Did you ever cut school? I inquired.

"A lot." She replied and I was surprised because she told me that she had good attendance for the most part.

"Okay. Why were you cutting school?"

"I just didn't feel like going them days, cause I wanted to hang out," she said nonchalantly.

"So who would you hang out with?"

"Cousins," she said, as they were her only friends.

"And what kind of stuff did you all do?"

"Just kick it, just hanging out in the house. Everybody's mother was working." I know that "kicking it" means a lot of different things, depending on who one asks, so she explained.

"So was that at your house?"

"Unh, unh. At they house. Sometime, we had other people over. Sometime drinking...we didn't do a lot of drinking. Playing cards, sleep, eat, just chilling, just laying back."

"Are there any particular days that you would cut school?"

"It wasn't no particular days, just cut when we felt like it."

"What did the school do when you cut classes?"

"Send letters. They called too."

"So what did your grandmother do when she found out?"

"She didn't never get the phone calls. I got the phone calls. Then they was sending out letters too. I got the mail. We was on top of it." Therefore, her grandmother was not aware of her cutting school.

"What did they do when they finally found out you were out of school?"

"That was around the time I had my baby." So it seemed that they were more concerned about her pregnancy then the school attendance at that time.

"Oh, that's right. Do you feel like anyone cared about you cutting school or classes?"

"No."

Cutting School, in School: Study Hall

Oftentimes, when one thinks of a student cutting class, there is an assumption that the student is not at school. This assumption would be incorrect in Carmella's case; in fact she cut class inside the school. She describes study hall as being the class of choice because it was the place to socialize. She described things that took place that were shocking, such as selling drugs, gambling, and so forth. It was unmonitored for the most part; teachers just came in to take attendance and left. She described study hall as the place to be, even if it wasn't her study period.

"It was a lot of gambling going on, it was a lot of drug selling in study hall. Study hall was the most popular thing in school. I'm serious." Carmella was responding to my laughter; I was laughing in disbelief. "Study hall 'cause that's where everybody hung out at."

"So people actually went to their study hall?" I asked because from my own high school experience and my experience as a teacher, students often cut study hall.

"Right. People actually went to study hall. I went to study hall. Back then West was popular for study hall. 'Cause you go in there and you see everything going on in study hall.

"That's where it was, study hall. Our study hall, the teachers would come and sign your work. This is what it was supposed to been, they'll come sign your work and no talking, no nothing, sign your work and they go and tend to do something else. At West it was okay for them to leave us in study hall cause they would walk pass and see what are you doing and we always closed the door. So, whoever on the outside, how they gone know it's not no teacher on the inside? Reefer was smoking, drugs was being sold, dice games, everything."

"What did you do in study hall?" I questioned as I wondered how she contributed to the scene.

"Hustling, selling weed. So that's where they found me at, in the study hall. I was in there way more than what I was supposed to be. Cut classes and sit in study hall. [There] used to be a lot 'cause see, we had like two classrooms in study hall. Plus the people that didn't supposed to be in there."

The Teachers

Carmella had both positive and negative experiences with her teachers. One of her most positive experiences with a teacher, Ms. Simpson, will be described in detail later. However, she also had negative experiences with some teachers. She described the duality of her interactions with teachers and also her impressions of them.

When asked about the teachers at her high school she replied, "They [teachers] was putting out a lot of good, but who took heed to it?"

"How do you think teacher felt working at West? Did they seem committed to being there?"

"It was they job. It was their bread and butter. If they had a choice to get bread and butter somewhere else, I think they would have. I don't think they really cared too much for being at West 'cause it was a lot going on."

Carmella did not feel that the teachers were truly committed to the students; she felt as though many of them were simply collecting a paycheck. In fact, she revealed something that I found very shocking. She told me that many of the teachers were working at the school, but were involved in either using or dealing drugs on the side.

"You know what, Cynthia, back in those days it was so much money out here in the community, half of the teachers was involved with it anyway. They worked a 9-to-5 just for a paycheck, just so when they go into a car lot and put this certain amount of money, the majority of that money is drug money. Some form of their family members is involved. The only thing that's saving them is a paycheck 'cause they can show, 'I work.' A lot of teachers was hustling in the community. It was common knowledge. The game, I know 'cause back then my family had the west side. My dad did, so he came in contact with them. I done seen the lawyers come, I done seen the police come to buy nice qualities from my daddy. So teachers, nurses, I mean people with professional jobs that that part of life is not supposed to be involved with they life. I mean professional-wise people, you know what I'm saying. Police is supposed to serve and protect. This teacher, 'You can't tell me things.' They can't."

I was appalled by this and I wondered how she could respect a teacher who she knew was involved in drugs, "So how did that make you feel about teachers since you saw them involved in the hustle too?"

To my surprise, she said she still respected them at school. "I'm gone still respect them because a lot of them that was working at the high school, I was seeing them on a regular basis after school. After school, I'm just saying."

"Did they live in the community? Why did you see them?"

"My father, 'cause they was buying drugs, my father."

"So they didn't even live there, they were just there getting stuff?"

"Right. My father, he was like you have to go, well he had these houses you would go into and I have came in a many of times and seen them. 'Hello,' that's the only thing I can say."

"How did you still respect them as a teacher though? I can imagine that would kind of make you feel like..."

"Yeah it did, but I mean I told my daddy, [He said] 'Keep your mouth closed.' I was supposed to keep my mouth closed. It was like what you see, you don't have to reveal."

"Were any of those your teachers?"

"Yeah, yeah."

"How do you respect somebody like that in the classroom?"

"It had happened when I got into a conflict with one of them and I knew, he been up all night and snapped out. I waited and I held it all in 'cause I knew he was coming back to see my dad again and my daddy gone take care of it. You know, so I knew not to just bust this teacher out because I could have just simply, back then I knew how to make a person lose their job. All I had to do is say drop this individual, drop them. They was gone be fired. You know what I mean?"

Ms. Simpson

Though Carmella did not get along with many of her teachers, there was one that had a positive impact on her, Ms. Simpson. She reflected upon the days when she had her as her dance teacher.

"Ms. Simpson, she was a dance teacher and I liked her because she was so different. She dressed weird, a weird person. She was weird to me and I liked her. Ms. Simpson, she was an older lady. She taught my aunties n'em, she taught my mama n'em. And she was still there when I got there. You know I was expecting her to be retired or something. They always used to tell me about Ms. Simpson. And I finally got a class with Ms. Simpson. It was a dance therapy class. But then she was teaching mathematics too, but I had her for dance. And I was excited everyday at sixth period. I was going to Ms. Simpson's class. That was the only part of my day that was okay. All my other teachers were just normal teachers. I didn't find nothing exciting about them. I didn't like them, they didn't like me. I didn't have to like them and they didn't have to teach me what I had to be taught and that was it. Yeah, Ms. Simpson was somebody you would go and talk to. [I talked to her] all the time about things that was like going on at home. She gave me good advice, what to do, what to say with my son's father, what to do, what to say, how to act, how to react. And I used to take her advice and every time I always used to come out right. I had her for ninth grade, tenth, and eleventh grade, all for dance. It was sixth period. Everybody liked Ms. Simpson. Her classroom just stayed crowded up for advice."

Transition into Prostitution: "My Baby Didn't Have No Pampers and No Milk"

Carmella was exposed to prostitution at an early age. She was 14 years old when she realized that her aunt was a prostitute. It was also around that age that she found out that her father was a pimp. "My daddy had a lot of prostitutes. So I been known about the game. So I knew about the game at a young age."

"At the time what did prostituting seem like to you?"

"At that time I used to, as I can remember, I used to just knew that they made money."

"Did you know exactly what was going on?"

"I was raised up with the game period, the pimping. My daddy was a pimp. I knew. My uncles n'em was pimps and I knew when I used to see the women and the houses we were in, I was like, I was the one that lingered on with the adults."

Though her father and uncles were involved in the prostitution industry, she was not introduced into it by them. I once asked her how she thought girls came into prostitution and she told me that it is usually by a man with whom they are in a relationship. This was true for her as well. She was told to start prostituting when she was 16. By that age, she had just had her son, and his father was in prison. She met an older man and started to date him; he started her to working the streets.

"I didn't actually stand on the corner. One time, maybe twice. [I was] 16 and dealing with an older guy, to get some money. Yeah, he told me to stand on the corner. This was after I had my son. He used to beat me a lot."

I asked her to tell me the story of how she first met this man because I wanted to know how he recruited her.

"He used to be hanging around our house all the time [her grandmother's house]. He was 23, 24 at the most. And uh, that was a bad mistake. That was another bad choice. I was pregnant with my son and he became my boyfriend. I was like two, three months when I started talking to him. And he just, whew I thought that was the way of life. He beat me. He was a good person far as like, I used to have to go to the doctor, stuff like that with my pregnancy he used to go with me and give me money and stuff like that but he was using drugs and I did not know. He was good to me until I had my baby. After I had my baby he was like, 'This is the way of life.' [He gave me] clothes, food, money. I stayed with my grandmother, so he spends the night. He comes over a lot, you know what I mean? So, after I had my baby we went to the projects. He wanted to, his family members stayed there so that's where he moved me to. He told me to leave too. My son was like a couple of months so we moved to the projects and it started from there, the drugs, prostitution, everything."

I asked her to tell me about the financial situation she was in when she first started and she described one of dire need.

"My son didn't have no milk and no Pampers so I asked him. He was like, 'It's time for you to get out and do something.' I don't have no job, what am I going to do? It's a job you can do, prostitution. So he took me to the area. He took me there and told me when a car pull up, they gone want something. The first time, he told me different prices for different stuff. So the first time a car pulled up, it was some cops, the very first time. When they pulled up he was like sitting across the street and you know I was walking down the street, the strip, and uh, man he pulled up and was like uh, a blow job. I was like, 'It's $40.' [He said] '$40, I got $30.' I was like, 'Damn, that's good enough.' I get in and handcuffs, there it go. They [the police] chased him [the boyfriend], they caught him. I was so scared. They chased him down, they beat him so bad. He stayed in jail overnight and I got out, he got out, that was it. 'I'm not going back there and stand down there.' He like, 'Oh yes you is, we going back.' [I said] 'Oh, no we not.' So he beat me, beat me tried to throw me off the 'L' platform [a subway train] and the 'L' was coming. So, [I said], 'Is there nothing different we could try, can't they come down here where we at?' It went like that. Like I always had this like Coca-Cola body shape. I still got it here today. So it was like I was a pretty girl and boys always liked me and this and that. So I sleep with them to get money. We never went back down there. I worked from home or around the house."

So after a time or two on the streets, she began to work at home or around their house. Soon, she had a clientele and worked as a call girl of sorts, with the customers coming to her house or going out with them. That is the arrangement that she started then and continued, even during the course of the time I interviewed her.

"So how would you get clients or customers?"

"They'd be coming through that area. It was more like I'd just go outside and put on me something real cute or whatever, walk to the store or something. I could pick up a date from there."

When Carmella's family heard about her prostituting, they came to take her home.

"After momma came and got me I knew that wasn't the way to live, like that."

"How long had you been down there, at that point? How long would you say you were out there?" I asked.

"I say like a good three months."

"Did you ever want to get out or how were you reacting to that?"

"He beat me, I'm like, 'Naw, I'm not gone do it, I'm gone go with your sisters n'em to sell drugs.' His sisters n'em go sell drugs, while he want me to sell this, my body. Uh-uh. I'm going with your sisters n'em to sell drugs."

Again, she mentioned that she was selling drugs. "You were doing both of them? So all the time your son was with you, right?"

She explained, "Mama had came and got him, took him to a safe environment—cleaner, back home until she had to come pick me up. She had to come pick me up 'cause he was beating me a little bit too much. And then he would have me walking around in public like, oh well, with two black eyes, broke arm."

"Were you still working during that whole time?"

"Not selling my body, I stopped. I was just hustling on the drug side. And that was it. After I got back with my mama, then he went to the penitentiary. He went for robbery."

I began to wonder if this man was pimping a lot of women or was she the only one. "Were you the only woman he had like that or did he have other girls?"

"I think I was the only one. Unless he had some undercover ones I didn't know about."

"Would you say you were making a lot of money? Were you making enough to take care of things since you said you didn't have money for Pampers or things like that?"

"The first time I went out to get it, I got busted by the police, then I made hundreds of dollars. We split the money."

No Pimp

Carmella was not one for giving her money to a pimp. She was what is known as a "renegade" prostitute, one who learns the rules of operation through street prostitution but eventually works without a pimp; I also refer to them as "pimpless prostitutes" (Williamson, 1999). Even when she first started at 16, she split the money with him. She never gave all her money to a pimp as many prostitutes do. As we will see later, she thought giving all her money to a man was a stupid and ridiculous concept.

"This my money. And I realized that a guy will pimp you and I have to define the meaning of the word pimp. What I call pimping is I have to give him some of the money.

"So as I got older I figured out what pimping was about. My son pimps me now. I have a pimp, it's my son though. Because if I'm making any money, I got to split it with him. He need Timberland boots, he need this, he need games, he need this, and he need that. So when I go to sleep [with a man], he's pimping me now. I gots to give it to him [the money]. I'm not gone give it to no man for them to do what they want to do with it. Buy some drugs, do this and do that, hell naw."

I was surprised to hear Carmella liken her son to a pimp; however, she meant it figuratively since she views pimping as an activity where a man gets money from a woman for sexual work that she had done. "Do you feel better about that though? Do you see a difference between your son and those men who pimp?"

"Yeah," she answered, clarifying her point.

"So is this going to good use or not?"

"This going to good use."

"Okay, so it doesn't bother you to give it to your son?"

"Naw, Naw, no, Uh-uh. And I have to learn that over the years."

"Right to This Day, I Still Do This": Still Prostituting

After Carmella's first introduction into prostitution by her boyfriend, she moved back to her grandmother's house and started working for McDonald's again. However, she did begin prostituting again, this time without a pimp. She was a little older and wiser, as it related to the industry. She had become a master at what she calls, "the game."

"Right, after getting away from him and I hadn't did it, I went into a new relationship and I started back when I was like 18 and 19 'cause I had to take care of my son. So, my mama, they was giving me money but they money wasn't good enough, I wanted more. Got a job, that wasn't good enough. I knew I had this body and I knew I could get paid for this body. So at 18, 19, I started back. I ain't have no pimp. If that's what you want to call it, I knew he was locked up and I didn't have nobody to stop me. So I knew hey, all my money I could make, it could just be for me and my son. I ran my own show. I knew I had this body, everywhere I go men was flirting with me. And the whole nine, 'Ooh, you look good' and this and that. 'I'll give you a couple of hundred, let's go out.' So, me and being brought up around money, [I would say] 'You have to pay for my babysitter.' [The men would say] 'How much your babysitter charge?' [I would reply] '$50.' They give it to me. So I knew then if I use what I got, I can get what I want. And I used it."

"So were you on the corner at this point?" I asked her and she shook her head indicating no. "Okay, so now your game is different because people are approaching you?"

"Yeah, they approaching me so I just tax them like I do right today. I still do this right today. It's nothing different that done happened in all the years, I'm 25 right now, nothing different. Then I say okay, I'm gone get my own business going. My cell phone, have my house phone, have my pager. All colors. It wasn't just no Black men, all races."

This time, she had a totally different way of prostituting, in which she met men and then told them they had to pay. She didn't stand on the corner. She saw it as charging men for what they usually get from women for free.

"Right to this day I still do this [prostitution], but I splits it with my son. I don't go out, they come to me. I have friends; I have a lot of male friends. I mean I have a lot of them. So, that's all. I, they never, men, right to this day, they never wanted me for me. They never wanted me for me. [They wanted] my body, that's it. So I figure, as I got older and start learning things, start experiencing more things in life, I knew that this was what to do. They want me, they got to pay me. And I am entitled to tell them what I want."

Working Traditional Jobs, Supplementing with Prostitution

Though Carmella was involved in prostitution, she also worked traditional jobs. Most of her income came from prostituting, but she describes herself as always being employed.

"Oh, I kept a job. I kept a job. I was a cashier, mostly everything you name, I done did it for a job. I done worked at Wendy's, Montgomery Ward, McDonald's, Dominick's."

"So, all the while, when you had a job would you still prostitute to supplement your income or was it like when you were working you didn't prostitute?" I asked her to understand why she continued to prostitute when she had a job.

"Oh, I still kept that going. 'Cause the more money I was getting, the more I could spend. My good days used to be when I was dealing with three friends. They were some big-time peoples. They knew each other. $3500. This came from like, one individual gave me $1000 and so on. And I'd be with three individuals in one night."

"That's a lot of money. Did you have to split that money with anybody or was that your money?"

"This is my money," she emphasized.

In Control of Her Own "Game"

Over the years, Carmella had learned that she needed to be in control of how she used her body to make money and who she shared that money with. At the time when she was involved in prostitution, she felt very in control. Since she viewed men as only wanting her body, she decided how she would broker it. Having the ability to charge for what most women give for "free," made her feel in control. She thought of it as a game. She told men what they wanted to her, gave them what they wanted, and they paid. She described the way in which she operated.

"So I got a job every two weeks, check coming in. I pulling a little public aid check, I'm gone sell me a little drugs, and I'm gone prostitute just to keep my rent paid. Just to keep my house, when somebody [a client] step in my house I want them to say, 'Damn, you got a nice crib.' That's good for business. Once they know I'm not cheap, it ain't no 20 dollars. No. I never slept with somebody for under $50. An average night, a couple hundred."

To get an idea of how things had changed since she was first forced to start as a frightened 16-year-old, I asked, "When you were 16 and you were with the guy, it was people you didn't know. It sounds to me like you moved to a point where you had a clientele, people you knew. Right?" She nodded her head. "Where would you meet these people?"

"'Cause I'm the type of person, I like to go places. I meet people wherever I go, wherever I go, I'm always meeting a man, two, three, four, five. They want a date, this is what I charge for the first 15 minutes and it don't take no cigarette 15 minutes to burn out. So by the time my cigarette is out, you gots to be out. I need 200 dollars."

"So if you meet somebody he becomes part of your clientele?" I asked to get a better understanding.

"If they on, if they looking for a date. Far as, they could just be wanting to go out and eat, I don't have time for that. Like I tell them, I shut them down as of now. I don't have time for it. 'What could you do for me? 'Cause I could feed myself, I can pay my own bills, I could do all that. What could you do for me?' Right now at this point that I can't do. Can you give me $300 right now to put in my pocket? Then I can go out and date you, we can go out to eat."

"You can go eat if you know first?" I asked, because it sounded like she didn't go out with men unless she would be paid for it.

"Yeah, can you do something for me at this point. I'm not finna [about to] just go sit at no restaurant and talk and all of that. For what? I can go home whip up my own food. I could go to my own restaurant."

Carmella described a financial situation with the men who she "dealt with" as them taking care of her needs by either giving her cash or paying for her expenses. She owned a two flat building where one of her men paid the mortgage, "I have certain clients...have their own businesses and I can get them to give me what I want. Things like a car, mortgage note paid." She saw herself as manipulating these men to give her want she wanted, summarizing men by stating, "You can get a man to do whatever it is you want to, all you have to do is just mold them."

Though she gave a picture of herself as being empowered and in control, brokering her body, she admitted that sometimes she was the one in need and at the discretion of her clients, like the predicament she was in when I met her. She was staying with her grandmother in the basement apartment because she was breaking up with her husband (her boyfriend whom she called her husband) and didn't want him to be able to contact her at her apartment building. She was in a financial pinch. She felt that she had to rely on her clients or "friends" more than she was comfortable with, "I have to keep flipping my script. You see what I'm saying. So right now I need them to cater to me now. 'Cause I can't care for myself the way I need to."

Carmella describes these men as "sweet vics", meaning that they can be controlled by women. However, she does express guilt about using guys for money who really like her. These are the men that give her money or take care of her needs that she does not sleep with; they just enjoy her company.

"It's all in the bedroom. What you put on, how you take it off. It's all sorts of little things. So this is how I've been surviving. Then you can get the credit cards and go through they bank accounts. You can get, right now what I'm getting. 'God please forgive me but you know I need this money.' So I have friends like that too, that I haven't never slept with that will go and buy me a brand new car."

Addicted to Drugs

Carmella has been a drug user for years, as she was introduced to major drugs when she was 16 by the boyfriend that started her to prostituting. She heavily used cocaine and heroin, though the latter was her drug of choice. "Yeah, I did heroin for 13 years. 13 years I did heroin. And I mean I wasn't settling for less." However, she never prostituted in exchange for drugs.

"So you never got to the point where you were prostituting for a fix? You would always get money?"

"Yeah. 'Cause I can go and buy my own drugs. I knew I had a drug habit, I was gone take care of that—mandatory."

"How much a day would you say your drug habit was? To put a dollar figure on it."

"A dollar figure, $500 to $600 a day."

Though she spent many years on drugs, she has been clean for years now, "I've been clean 35 months." It is because of her struggle with drugs that she wants to be a drug counselor. She told me that she didn't really feel in control of herself or able to deal with her problems until she was free of drugs and got psychological counseling. She told me that her ideal job was that of a drug counselor because she wanted to help other women reclaim themselves and their lives.

The Money and the Things

When Carmella first began prostituting, it was because she needed money to take care of her son. She needed the money to survive. However, after starting again at 18 with a drug habit, she was also addicted to the money. She had gotten accustomed to a certain lifestyle, "I was addicted to getting the money. It's like I couldn't live without turning a date, everyday turning a date. Two, three, four, five dates and the money. So I was attracted to it. You get accustomed to it. If you trick off with different individuals everyday, two, three, four times a day, you get accustomed to it, very addicted to it. I was addicted to the money."

She described her spending habits with me, "Just like some days, I might go make $300. But once I go do what I have to do, it's like, I'll spend $300 on me, a pair of boots and I'm broke. I don't even have the money for my cigarettes 'cause they all going on one pair of boots. I can't do that, not right now. So it's like what I get now, I have to pinch off that."

Carmella spent an excessive amount of money, even she admits that. However, she did have the wherewithal to purchase a building. At the time I met her, her attitude about money had changed. As she stated above, she realized that she couldn't spend $300 on boots if it left her with no money. Also, she believed, "If you take the hustling money and put all that money to a business, that's the only way you gonna make it. It's like this money here [she was speaking figuratively], if you go make $100,000 and you take half and spend it on a car...The other half, if you got an apartment you gotta pay rent, you gotta dress this car out the way you want it, clothes, you broke. $50,000 car, the other 10 on clothes, the other 10 you just jagged on drinking and smoking or whatever, you got 30 left, you ain't got none left."

Getting Out, Wanting to Stay Out

When I first started working with Carmella, she was still prostituting. However, during the course of us working together, she stopped again. Over the years she had stopped and started a few times. She simply got tired of it, "You get tired. You got to have a downfall."

"What would you say was yours? What finally made you tired?" I asked.

"Dealing with the individuals. Dealing with these people, all these different individuals, all these different personalities. I knew once if I stopped the drugging, everything else was gone have to stop. I was just tired of it. I was just tired of everything."

On another occasion when we were talking about things that she would change in her life if she could, she replied, "All the men that I have been involved with. Go back and get all my sex back, I abused my body. I used it bad." She clearly regretted prostituting and the effects it had on her.

At the time when she started prostituting, she felt as though she didn't have a choice, but now that she had stopped, she reflected on other choices she could have made, "I didn't have to sell my body anyway, my mom and dad had plenty of money but I knew if this individual wanted to get up with me, he had to pay. I just chose to be grown before my time. I had other options but that was the easiest way out. That was the quickest way to me. And I hate to say it, today I'm not like that anymore, but it's still the quickest way out there. I didn't have to do it. [I could have] continued to work a job."

She clearly regretted it because when I commented on the amount of money she made and asked her what else could she have done to make that amount of money, she told me that working a job wasn't paying her the kind of money that she needed, "...but I could've just waited. Eventually the money would have gotten better, but I wanted it right away....[I could have] got two jobs, work long, more hours." Today, as an older, more mature women who had made what she terms "bad decisions", she thought anything would have been better than prostituting. In hindsight everything seems clearer, but it didn't when she was 16 and it didn't seem so clear when I first met her, just three months earlier.

By the time we were finishing the study, Carmella had come to the conclusion that illegal activity, both dealing drugs and prostituting, wasn't worth the money. The money made from prostituting wasn't worth her "using" her body. And the time she had spent in jail wasn't worth the money. She recently had spent 39 days in jail and said she thought she was going to die that time. She just couldn't go back. The used feeling from prostituting and the jail time from drug dealing made her decide that she would take the straight and narrow. She was looking for a job when I last talked to her.

Carmella's Community: "Gangs and Drugs"

Carmella grew up on the west side of Chicago, in an impoverished socioeconomic area infamous for high levels of crime and dilapidated property. Empty lots where houses once stood are a common sight. I asked Carmella to describe the community in which she grew up and she summed it up in two words, "Gangs and drugs." She said that it was not the kind of community in which she would like to raise her son, though he was 12 and had lived there with her grandmother for a nice part of his life. It was a community absent of businesses and where shootings and drug use and selling were common. The only businesses in her community were corner stores. I asked if there were any service agencies in the area and the only one that she named was Planned Parenthood; however, she said she never used their services. In order to live in her community she said that one needed to know, "how to hustle and that's how to survive. It's right there, how to hustle."

School and the Community

For the most part, Carmella's school was not involved in her community; they did not offer community outreach services. The school was an entity in and of itself. Though it provided medical services and day care for girls with children, it did not go into the community or invite the community in, according to Carmella. The only contact that school personnel had with the community was unofficial and negative, as she earlier described teachers who were involved with the drug trade in the community both as dealers and users. She said that she never learned anything in school that related to her community.

When teachers did talk about the community, it was to advise students to do well in school so they could move away from it. What is interesting about her community is that it is now a Federal Empowerment Zone; that means that it is identified as a highly impoverished area, and receives funds from the government for rebuilding. It is undergoing gentrification, meaning that the government is giving tax breaks as incentives for businesses to move into the community. Also, houses are being built and taxes are being raised. Ironically, this crime-laden community will be a good neighborhood once again; however, most of its current residents, like Carmella's grandparents, probably won't be able to afford to live there because of the higher taxes.

Work and the Community

The community in which Carmella grew up has a high unemployment rate today; however, she said that many folks that she knew worked, though she did not know what they did. "I'm not aware of what the peoples did. I knew a lot of people that was working, had jobs." She knew that some of her family members worked, but she did not know in what capacity. I couldn't quite understand how she could live in a house with her family members and not know where they worked or what they did. So it seems as though careers and jobs was not something that was talked about; it was good to be employed at all.

When I asked her what women in her community did for work she replied, "I don't know. I wasn't ever the type of person to be in people's business 'cause I don't want nobody in mine, so I don't know what they did. I don't know what they did. All I knew was what my household was doing and my cousins' household and stuff like that. I knew the teenagers that was hanging out, I didn't know what they mothers did. All I knew if I go over they house, they mother n'em gone. You know what I mean? My momma at work that's all they used to say."

The Community's Idea of Success

Since she didn't describe people in the community as having careers or have any knowledge about what they did for work if they worked at all, I wanted to get a clear understanding of the way in which the community characterized success. I wanted to know if the drug dealing was frowned upon or something to aspire to and what they thought about the unemployment. "According to the community you grew up in, what does a person have to have or do to be considered successful?"

"Get out the community. Get out the community," she said.

"And then once you left, the people thought that you made it?"

"Right, 'cause if you stayed in that community, it was only a couple of things you could do, sell drugs, prostitute, get a little job."

"Okay. So like the people who were hustling, making it big, and had whatever, were they considered successful by the people in the community or were people like, 'It's a shame what Joe is doing.' Did people look up to the folks who were hustling and getting their money on?"

"Naw."

"Nobody did? They didn't think that was a respectable way of living?"

"No, it's not, it wasn't, never will be."

"Well, some people do consider it as successful, that's why I'm saying. In your community was it considered successful?"

"No. Only if you apply a business to it. If you take the hustling money and put all that money to a business. That's the only way you gonna make it."

"Okay. Is that how you considered or did everybody in the community think that way? Is that your own opinion?"

"That would be mine and a lot of other people opinion too." Carmella was clear that illegal activity as work in the community was frowned upon and only respected if it was used to bolster a legal business.

The Family: "My Daddy Was A Rolling Stone"

Carmella grew up in a household with her extended family. Her grandparents owned the house, but her mother, aunts, and uncles lived there as well. She stated that there was so much traffic in her house that she would be cutting school at home and no one ever noticed because there were so many people in the house at a given time. During her childhood, she lived with her maternal grandmother, who reared her. In fact, she often referred to her grandmother as her mother.

Her Parents as Partners

Her parents were never married, "They lived together but they never was married." She stated that she remembered living in the house with both her parents when she was very young, "off and on." One of the reasons that they never lived together for long as a family unit is because of her father's lifestyle, as he was what she termed "a rolling stone." That meant that he had many women and lived for short lengths of time with all of them on a rolling basis. "By my daddy running the street and having so many families, you know what I mean, he's here, he's there off and on." I asked her how her mother felt about this and she said, "She always saw him, they partners. That's what they call each other, partners." They still have a relationship today, they simply have an understanding that it is an open relationship.

"My Daddy was a Pimp"

After a of couple interviews, Carmella revealed that her father was pimp, and that is how she first learned about prostitution. "The women that my father had around him, my daddy had a lot of prostitutes. So I been known about the game. So I knew about the game at a young age. I was raised up with the game period, the pimping. My daddy was a pimp. My uncles n'em was pimps and I knew when I used to see the women and the houses we were in I was like, I was the one that lingered on with the adults."

She spoke about her father on many occasions. "I ain't never seen my father with a job. If he did, it was like when he was like 15 or 16. I think he had a job when he was like 15 or 16. He like 45, 46 years old—my daddy was a rolling stone, hustler, pimp. He is a smart-ass man. He could tell you about every part on your body, better than a doctor can. He studied a lot of medical [things], but he didn't go into the field. He studied at home as far as reading books and stuff like that. But he didn't take no type of classes or nothing. You know what I mean, that he could have benefited from. He know how to do a lot of things. He's a smart man. Wherever he lay his hat is his home. But he still living. Money was his lifestyle."

"Is he still into it?" I asked.

"Uh-huh. Yeah."

"You think he's doing good? Is his hustle working for him?"

"I guess so."

"Is he taken care of pretty good?"

"His wife make a pretty good piece of money."

"Oh, so he's kind of settled now?"

"Yeah, but he still got different women. He's still real volatile."

He was also involved in drugs, "He also was involved in dealing drugs, along with his brothers." He dealt drugs in the community and had earned the fear and respect of the people.

She did not describe her relationship with her father; she stated that she was closest to her mom.

Her Mother

Carmella is close to her mother, though she used to be closer to her than she is now. Her mom lived in the house with her, but there were times when she was not present. Carmella said that during the time when her next-door neighbor molested her, she wasn't involved in her life much. Even though her mother was not always there as much as she could have been, she still loves and respects her. Her mother's support was very important as she recovered from the incident. In fact, her mother was the only one she told that he had raped her, "I told my mother. At this point and time she was involved with the streets real heavy. So I think if she was there, during that time then this wouldn't have happened, I think. Her and my daddy was involved with the streets real heavy. Dealing drugs and using them." My mom, yeah, I used to be real, real close to her for many years. I used to be real close to her cause I was the only child. She went to church, she took good care of me. But, I ain't never seen her with no job for many years, five years straight. I can recall my mother having one or two jobs taking care of older people, she had a good heart, she was sweet."

"I Love My Son"

Carmella had her son when she was 16 years old. It was because of her inability to provide for him, that she didn't have any milk or Pampers for him, that she prostituted for the first time. She loves her son very much. She is very proud of him and brags about how smart he is and her hopes for his future. When she got to a point where she couldn't take care of him or had him in an unsafe environment, she would take him to her mother. She tries to keep her activities from her son. She describes how she handled clients coming over to her house. I asked her about safety and about her son being there.

"If they have to come to my house, I mean I take chances 'cause I bring them to my house. But, my son, he never sees me. He never...I always got it so he can't see nothing.

"He know I got a lot of male friends, but he don't, like, *know* [italics added]. He call me a pimp. My son calls me a pimp. He say, Mama, you use men for they money. I say, I shoul' do. I say that's to help us. He say okay. As he long as when Friday come and he did good in school all week, on Friday he can check him $200 to $300 to go shopping and grab him something, he don't say nothing. Unless he can go showboat and say look I spent this much on this and that."

Carmella's Closest Family Relationship

Carmella has been through a lot in her life. As someone who has struggled with drug abuse and prostitution, she has broken a lot of promises. She has tried to start over many times. After disappointing herself and her family, they started not to believe in her. Her aunt is the one person who still does, who believes she can turn her life around once and for all. I asked her whom she is the closest to and she told me about her aunt who she loves and respects, "My auntie, she graduated. She went to the same high school. And I was always told that education is very important as far as making money. I'm telling my son that it is really important. That's why I went back and got my G.E.D. My auntie was a good role model because she got her high school diploma and I wanted that."

"Who you trust most? I asked.

"My auntie Sheila. I trust her 'cause she ain't never let me down."

"What was the biggest jam you were in that she helped you out of?"

"The situation I'm in right now. 'Cause she took me and my husband in. And she got my back and she believe in me. She know I can do it. When my other part of the family, they don't think I can."

"She the only one that's still holding out hope for you?"

"Yep."

"Do you ever feel like you don't want to let her down? Do you worry about that?"

"Uh-uh."

The Men in Her Personal Life

The molestation that Carmella experienced was extremely traumatic to her, and it has colored the way she feels about men and the way she interacts with them. As a result, she has not been able to enjoy an intimate relationship with a man. Even her most intimate relationships with her boyfriends, who she referred to as husbands because she has never been legally married, lacked intimacy, "I never got no pleasure out of none of it. Every time I've laid down, I'm like ooh, God, I'll be glad when this is over with. I take my mind somewhere else. I take me somewhere else. And I, even with boyfriends, relationships, whatever, my relationships six-, seven-month relationships, but whatever the case maybe I always feel like that."

"So, have you ever been in love or in a relationship where you felt like you wanted more out of it than the money? Or like you said every time you lay down you feel like, 'I hope this is over.' Have you always felt like that, even when you were married?"

"Uh-huh, even when I was married. And my husbands, they knew about my past. I don't know. They knew when I was feeling like that. And I just say hey, just leave it alone. You know what I mean? Leave me alone."

She still thinks that men only want her for what she provides sexually, even in relationships that are not business. "...men right to this day, they never wanted me for me. And that's why, even though I have been married twice [she's never been married legally but has lived with men in what she terms marriages], my son's father and the guy I just divorced. They never wanted me for me."

"What do you think they wanted you for?" I asked.

"My body, that's it."

The Psychological

The Molestation

"But before I made it into high school, I was molested and that kinda changed my life—that did change my life. [I was molested by my] next door neighbor. [It happened] one time. I became pregnant, so he took my virginity away from me. I think if he hadn't did that I probably would still probably be a virgin I think. You know, so I looked at men different."

"You said you looked at men different for a while. And how would you describe how that affected the way you looked at men?"

"They taking it from you. I looked at it like, I know this is not the way it's supposed to be. When you say no, you say no and that stuck with me for many years, even now. It's still affecting me, with me, I still don't look at them the same."

"Did it change the way you looked at yourself or like the world around you?"

"Yeah. It took effect on me. 'Cause it's like I didn't care."

"Did anyone know about it?"

"No, not for like three months...."

"So your mother wasn't at home a lot. So the person that did this, was he an older person?"

"I was 13 and he was about...he was grown, good and grown."

"And how did your mother react?"

"She took me out of school. He was still living at the time, after he did this. And he used to like threaten me. He died eventually. He used to like threaten me, I better not tell nobody or he gone kill me. He gone do it again. He used to be like umm, saying all kind of dirty mean stuff to me and have me scared to tell somebody. You understand what I mean? And by me being, you know, I bet not tell 'cause he gone hurt me if I do, I stopped going to school, they used to be thinking I was going to school but I really wasn't. By my grandmother's house being as big as it was, everyone was occupied and they didn't know if I was in the house or not. It was a big house and I used to hide in the basement. So that was it—days and days and days were going by and I wasn't in school, they used to call. My uncle used to be like go to the store. I would never go to the store. I used to just get the money and hide up in the front room or in the hallway somewhere and I'd be like somebody snatched you money out my hand and I used to have to keep the money. I didn't want to but that kept me from me going outside."

"Did you eventually do anything with the money?"

"Yeah, like I told my mom and she moved me to the hotel for a while, we stayed in a hotel for a while, I got an abortion and all of this, but uh, then they found out the reason why I wasn't going to the store, going to school and things like that. They all put it together. Then it was something did about it, it was something did about it. But he, [and all] men now, I mean for a long time I was just you know, used to just scare me so much. It's like every time I opened up the window he would be there. And then know I'm coming in and if I'm in the window he would look at me real mean or something. You know, and then finally, you know after my family, my mom, knew about it. Things started changing. Things started changing, my life just changed. I don't know, I wish I could go back because all the things I know now, I could have used them. Men, they always took advantage of me like, they like, that's what they did.

Dealing with Molestation

"[The attitude] came after I got molested. That's what's been following me all those years. My attitude, I just started working on the attitude. I just started working on it."

"Have you ever had counseling for it?"

"Uh-huh. 14 all the way until now.

"Would you say that it helped?"

"Yeah, 'cause I opened up. I just learned how to talk about [it] two years ago. If I didn't learn how to talk, you wouldn't be sitting here having a conversation with me. I know how to talk. That's why I want to be a counselor.

Hope for Tomorrow: "See My Faith Is Really Big"

Ideal Program

I told Carmella that I was conducting this study to create research that would help schools create programs to help girls who are on the fringes of dropping out, and to help create alternative programs for those who have already dropped out and entered a lifestyle such as the one she has been involved in. So I asked her about how she thought a program such as that could be designed.

"If you could make like a program for young girls, especially the young ones who drop out of school and stuff like that, a program to help them, what would it be like? What do you think would need to be in that program?"

"Drug counseling, emotional counseling, support groups. Aw, my program would be off the hook. I think I could save a lot of women."

This desire to help women like herself led her to wanting to go back to school to become a drug counselor. "It [education] is important now because I want to go back to school. I want to be a drug counselor."

"Why do you want to be a drug counselor?"

"'Cause I have so much to offer. 'Cause I done seen everything, I been there, done it, so I have a testimony and I want to give back, especially to the women that's locked up and they feel they can't make it."

Because she had such faith that she could help women, I asked her to continue to describe her program, "What would be in your program?"

"I mean, a real life. And what I mean by that, everything you looking for would be in this program. School, education-wise, help getting your children back, working on self, putting God first and it would be so much, the first thing they gone do is find God cause he is the only man, the only person on this Earth who can help you turn your life around. And once I can give to them what I help them to learn, they don't have no choice than to turn it around. They don't have no choice but wanting to do the right thing."

"If It Wasn't for God"

After all that she has been through, Carmella still has faith that her life can change and that she can have her dreams of a family and a life without prostitution and drugs. She remains optimistic, because she says that God has gotten her out of worse things, that he must have a plan for her life and that fuels her hopes. These are the last words she shared with me during our last interview.

"Do you feel like you're in control of your life?"

"Right now I'm not. 'Cause God is in control of my life. Every time I was in control I came out with nothing. So now he's got it. Every time I tried it my way it didn't work, every single time. Now this time I'm going by his way. I mean my mind is made up. This is what I have to do. And I ask God to give me strength. Give me my direction, give me my path and he guide my path and say okay, you go straight this way. If he say go straight I can not turn, 'cause if I turn to the left it's a dead end. Right, dead end, nothing. I'm gone run into a trap each way. I'm gone go straight. If I can go back and change, aw man."

"Do you know that even though you can't go back and change, everyday you wake up, it's your day to undo...do you see it that way?"

"Yeah, today I do. Oh, I can do it different. It's just that now I would...okay, like the drugs. I know that that can't be changed. The drug addiction, the drugs. I know that's only one resort and that is I go hustle and I'm going to jail, directly to jail."

"Are you on some sort of probation?"

"I'm on probation now and I'm going to court."

"For that same thing?"

"For that same thing. I go to court this month and I know that God got my back. And people really need to realize that there is a God. 'Cause if you pray for something and you open your heart and change your mind and your thinking, he'll do everything else. See, I made up in my mind now that I'm not gone sell any drugs and I ask God everyday and I kept talking to him like I'm talking to you and I asked and I received. On January 9th, he let me come home. I was losing my heart and I changed it. So I'm not out to use God, 'cause he can snatch me up and lock me back up. See, the devil still alive and if you don't put the blood of Jesus on you, Satan, he got you. And he stole my identity and the identity he took from me, I let him have it. But it's blood on it so he can't use my identity. He the one caused all this stuff to go on in my life. God had a path for me and the devil was there at the same time God had my path for me. I just went on down and meet him and stand out there with him. I went to that path and took that wrong curve and went down. And people really need to realize, I have a testimony, people need to realize, there is a God and a lot of people really don't see that. And I'm learning more about him 'cause he real. He's really real. And if you get closer to him, he'll change things in your life. He changed things in my life. Who you think brought me through the madness I been in? It was God, it wasn't nobody but God. If it wasn't for God, I'd have been dead a long time ago. He got me here for a reason."

"You know what that is yet?"

"I don't know, aw man I wish I knew what God got me here for. I don't know what the reason is. I asked to be back home and he let me come back home. Faith and believing. You can have faith of a mustard seed. That is a little tiny seed. That is a little seed. You have that much of faith. See my faith is really big. It's really big."

Understanding Carmella: An Interpretation

Carmella's life has been laden with challenges and obstacles, even at a young age. As I asked her to take me with her through the journey of her life, I often thought that it was nothing short of amazing that she had made it to the other side of some of the tragedies that had befallen her: periods of neglect by her parents, family involvement in crime, taunting and abuse by peers, molestation, physical abuse, teen pregnancy, drug addiction, imprisonment, and prostitution. Yet, she still stood as a testament to the resilience of the human spirit. Many days, I listened to her and thought, "So this is how it happens, it's no wonder." Much of the work done on adolescent prostitution indicates that many of these girls come from this type of background, and Carmella's life was no exception (Calhoun, Jurgens, & Chen, 1993; Ellenwood, 1991; Ivers & Carlson, 1987; Weisberg, 1985; Schaffer & DeBlassie, 1984; Silbert & Pines, 1982). However, before thinking "it's no wonder", the other three cases must be considered. There are two young women in the study who did not come from backgrounds which are considered to be the typical paths to dropping out and prostitution. Yet, some of the same themes that emerged in Carmella's case study are present in their cases as well; hence, these findings cannot be dismissed as relevant only to young women from socioeconomically challenged backgrounds.

The Social Dynamics of Schooling as an Impetus for Dropping Out

When I conceptualized this study as one that captured the in-school and nonschool educational experiences of young women dropouts who turn to prostitution for economic sustenance, I anticipated hearing stories and vivid memories from their classroom experience. I thought that a great deal of the in-school experience would stem from what took place in the classroom. I expected stories with rich detail about teachers, whether they were positive or negative experiences. Those stories were absent in Carmella's recounting of her school experience. I was so surprised about her lack of specific memories from the classroom, that I revisited questions I thought would spark her memory, because surely there must be some. Where and why was she hiding them? I was waiting to be transported there through her memories, but we never arrived, at least not there. I felt as though something was missing because things were not turning out as I had anticipated. After a reviewing field notes and transcripts repeatedly, it dawned on me: Carmella's in-school experiences in the classroom were unremarkable to her and had escaped the boundaries of her memory; instead, that space was occupied by the social dynamics of her in-school experience. For her, the in-school experience was not about the classroom, but about the social challenges she faced.

Carmella's conflicts with other girls at school started when she was in elementary school and continued and intensified through high school. These girls terrorized her—gangs of them sometimes physically attacked her—and it had driven her to a life of isolation at school. Because she was a loner, she didn't have much help when these confrontations ensued. These conflicts had colored her in-school experience, to the extent that they had *become* the experience. Upon review of my notes and transcripts, I realized that since the very first interview, she had been telling me vivid stories about her in-school experience; they just weren't the ones I expected. They were those that were salient to her; they were the stories of a girl who had to fight her way through school. One can only imagine how her experiences with her female peers must have negatively affected her motivation for attending and completing school. In fact, many students who drop out and/or are involved in delinquent activities were isolated and suffered a great deal of conflict at school (Jordan et al., 1994; Ellenwood, 1991).

Attitude as Standpoint Theorist

As Carmella recounted her story, I could see the frustration on her face and hear the tension in her voice. She seemed to have reached a point in her life where she had suffered as much misfortune as she could take. This was evident in the way she interacted at school, in her personal life, as well as with me. As she described her confrontations with her teachers, I knew that she was what many teachers would classify as a "problem" student, she was the student who would become insubordinate with little to no apparent motivation. She brought her disagreeable attitude with her to class and would spiral out of control on many occasions. Though she says that she was never kicked out of class due to her behavior, it is difficult to believe.

Some literature on female dropouts suggests that these girls are usually quiet in the classroom and go unnoticed because of their ability to avoid creating disruptions in the classrooms. As a result, the teachers do not seem to notice that they are first mentally and eventually physically withdrawing from school (Sadker & Sadker, 1994). Carmella was the antithesis of this type of dropout. Instead, she was loud and confrontational in class, as we see from the episode that took place between her and her White history teacher. She was "womanish", as Alice Walker describes this term: an African American girl who wants to be an adult and acts in ways that are not thought to be appropriate for a child (1983). It also refers to one who is politically aware. Her racial awareness and political views were shown when she stated that she did not understand why a White person was teaching Black people about slavery, echoing the tenets of positionality, i.e., who has the "right" and authority to speak about certain issues (Takacs, 2002; Maher & Tetreault, 2001).

Carmella's attitude was the focus of her counseling sessions for some years; she told me that was the only reason that she was able to participate in the study. On a couple of occasions, she seemed to be in an unpleasant mood when I arrived to interview her. In one interview, I could feel the tension when I entered her apartment. A few minutes into the interview, I noticed that she was answering all of the questions with simple yes or no responses. I asked her if she was okay or if she wanted to meet another time, but she insisted on continuing. Finally, she said that she could tell that I had never been involved in some of the things she had been, prostitution and drugs, and added that I probably would not be a good drug counselor because I lacked that experience. She added that she would be a great counselor and told me that counseling was her career aspiration. Her statement surprised me and I did not know how to respond to it, but it was true. I reminded her that my reason for working with her was to gain an understanding of how to meet the needs of young girls such as her, that she was telling her story in the service of preventing other young women from taking the same path. I also shared some of my own life challenges with her. After she had shared her views on how she felt about me, the outsider without experience in "street life," she seemed to feel better and her comfort level was restored. So just as she wondered about the history teacher's "right" to teach about African American slavery, she wondered about my "right" to write about the life of someone who had dropped out and was involved in street life.

That day I realized, though we were the same, both African American women close in age, we were very different. We occupied two very different standpoints: the African American woman of privilege nearing the end of a terminal degree who had never known street life, and the African American woman who lacked a traditional high school diploma and who had been entrenched in prostitution and drugs. Though we share some commonalities as Black women, we are not the same; hence, the validation of feminist standpoint theory (Hallstein, 2000; Collins, 1997; Hirschmann, 1997; Harstock, 1990b). These differences were extremely apparent to Carmella. I often wondered if she saw me as more akin to the White history teacher than to her because of my privilege.

Vacillating between the Empowered Woman and the Victim

When Carmella's boyfriend-turned-pimp first introduced her to prostitution, she was in financial straits, as she did not have money for her baby's basic needs. At that time, she described herself as a victim of a man who abused her and forced her to sell her body. A couple of years later, she began prostituting again, though this time she did not view herself as the victim, but rather as an empowered woman, "taxing" men for what they usually get for free (that is, sex). She began to see herself as the pimp and the men as her prey. In some of the interviews, she bragged about her ability to get men to do whatever she wanted and about how easy it was to manipulate them. In those interviews, she seemed to take on a different persona, and I was amazed at how elaborate her plans were for manipulating her clients. She was portraying herself as the empowered prostitute that many feminist theorists describe. She viewed her body as a commodity and sold it to those who needed her services. She saw it as a business transaction and her empowered persona was very convincing.

The next time I saw her, however, she had a different view, one that remained constant throughout the remainder of the study. She saw herself as the victim once again. She lamented over how she had "used and abused" her body and about how men have always wanted her for sex, even the men she terms as her "husbands". She told me that she thought since men took sex from her, as her next door neighbor did, she might as well get paid for giving it to them. She told me that she detested sex. On these occasions, she seemed depressed to me, talking slower, and in a lower tone. She was willing to do anything not to go back into prostitution and was desperately seeking legitimate employment. So she lived at the two extremes, the empowered prostitute and the victim. Carmella's vacillation between these two positions led me to agree with feminist theorists who posit that women who are the victims of molestation and rape as children are not empowered by brokering their bodies, but that they are victims who have turned their abuse inward (Russell, 1993; Wynter, 1987; Dworkin, 1987; Barry 1979).

Socioeconomic Despair

In the 1960s, Carmella's community was considered a safe and economically viable residential neighborhood; however, the community has undergone many changes since that time. In the 1960s the community was predominantly White working-to-middle class families. However, as people of color began moving into the area, White flight ensued, as the White families started to move out. Over the years, the community began to face challenges of high crime rates, including gang and drug infiltration, and unemployment (IWA, 2002; Loury, 2002). In past years, the community was home to many vacant houses and empty lots littered with debris. However, the community is rapidly changing as gentrification brings new homes and housing improvements to the area (Mannion, 1996). The neighborhood is now almost evenly balanced between African Americans and Latinos. While the area is improving, it continues to be plagued by the drug trade and violence.

Carmella and her family fell prey to the drug industry, as it was one of the primary sources of income for her family. As she stated, her family was known as the most prominent drug dealers in the community. She, as well as her family members, felt that they had few options for legitimate employment, due to a lack of education and skills. In her community, it is not unusual for people to be lured by the drug industry, since the unemployment rate in the area is one of the highest in the city of Chicago (Loury, 2002). The opportunity to make substantial amounts of money in short periods of time is irresistible for many, like Carmella, who find themselves involved in drugs and prostitution. As she once told me when I asked her about options for employment other than prostitution, "...that was the easiest way out, that was the easiest way to me. And I hate to say, today I'm not living like that anymore, but it's still the quickest way out there." In fact, the lure of the "quick money" is so strong in her community that it has the highest recidivism rate for drug-related offenders in Chicago (Loury, 2002). Violence is also prevalent in the community, so the deferred gratification of completing school and starting a career is not practical to them as they are painfully aware of their mortality each time someone falls victim to a deadly crime (Loury, 2002). As Carmella told me, she is constantly worried about her son being shot by a stray bullet.

Hearing Carmella's story and weighing her life experiences, I remain amazed at her resilience, at her willingness to try to live a life free of drugs and prostitution. I am encouraged by the fact that she has received her G.E.D. and has enrolled in a job-readiness program. Deep within, she remains committed to making a different life for herself and her son. Her struggles have not led to bitterness, but a willingness to help others in her predicament, as she wants to become a counselor and remained committed to this study, even in the midst of her trials.

CHAPTER SIX

Celina's Story: "I Can't See Myself Standing on No Corner"

I heard about Celina before I met her; one of the women I talked with about the study told me that they knew of another woman who might be interested in participating. She added that she was a "real" prostitute. When I asked her to define a "real" prostitute, she described the popular cultural notion of a woman with a pimp who trades and barters sex from street corners. She described her appearance, as she thought I surely must have seen her before, adding details about her unusual hair color and her stiletto boots. I must admit, her appearance was quite remarkable; though she was of dark completion, she wore a platinum-blonde hair weave. She wore tight blue jeans, and leopard-skin stiletto boots, about five inches high. I marveled at how well she could move in those heels; it was as if she were wearing flats. I knew that the agility and comfort she displayed came from practice, and upon talking with her I learned that she had years of practice, as she had been a prostitute for more than five years.

I told her about the study and that she had to be involved in prostitution to participate, and she readily told me that she had been a prostitute for many years, working for the same pimp. She said that she would be happy to help me. She was truly interested in helping other young women who were on the brink of entering her lifestyle. She was straightforward, open, and honest throughout the time that I spent with her. She never seemed to be uncomfortable or bashful about any of the things she shared with me. She was very thorough in all of her responses, to the extent that she required the least follow-up questions of all of the three informants. Celina had the uncanny ability to be descriptive to the extent that her words were like a brush on the canvas of her life. To hear her story was like being transported back to the actual event. She was a magnificent storyteller.

I told Celina that I needed her to create an alias, as I could not refer to her by her real name. She replied, "Oh, you can use (the name everyone called her) because that's an alias. You can use that name."

I was surprised because the name was a proper name and not a nickname. So, no one actually knew her real name, not the other women, and not me. That was the first thing that struck me about her; that it never occurred to her to share her birth name. That was the way she interacted with the world, as an assumed identity. I asked her to create another one and she quickly came up with Celina. She shared her background with me, and like Carmella, she grew up on the west side of Chicago in an area bustling with crime and socioeconomic despair.

"Well, I grew up on the west side of Chicago, my two brothers, my mom, my father. It was a normal childhood. To me it wasn't normal because as I got older, I know I wasn't living in a normal household, I was living is a dysfunctional household because my mother and father used to fight every weekend. My brothers n'em would leave and I used to beg them, 'Please don't leave because momma n'em gone start fighting.' And they like, 'No they not.' So I used to wake up to fights every weekend." So though her nuclear family was intact, with both of her parents living in the household, it was a violent and unpredictable home.

Though Celina grew up in a community where most of the residents were economically stressed, she describes her family's financial situation as one of abundance, but scarce on the family time. "My mother gave me the best of everything, but she wasn't there for me, you know the way I really wanted her to be there. It was always, 'Come Thursday we can go shopping and get whatever you want.' I got the best of everything, but she wasn't there for me.

You can't buy a child. You know what I'm saying? The child want that attention and she wasn't there for me with the attention I that I wanted."

Instead of being there to build the relationship with her children, her mother worked full-time and attended college courses at night. Celina never seemed to be able to recover from that lack of attention, as she frequently talked about her mother's absence. Therefore, her father gave her the attention she needed; today he remains the cornerstone in her life.

Because Celina lacked supervision, it was easy for her to withdraw from school without being immediately noticed. Though she valued education, her need for attention pulled her away from her studies and into activities that eventually led to her dropping out. Her parents never noticed that she was slipping away. In fact, she had been out of school for more than a month before her mother knew that she had stopped attending school.

Celina told an interesting story, as she was from a two-parent, financially-stable household with a mother who was college-educated. Though she had her son at 16, he was not her reason for dropping out, as she attended a high school for pregnant girls while she was expecting. She dropped out of school due to "boredom." She found her nonschool curriculum, i.e., hanging out with friends and drinking, more exciting.

Dropping Out: "If It Don't Interest Me, I Ain't Finna Try to Apply Myself to Do It"

Boredom with Traditional Subjects

Celina often found her classroom experience boring. It was difficult to stay focused because she did not see the connection between what she was learning in the classroom and her personal life and interests. She described typical days in class as droning on and without variety.

Though she did not like most of her traditional classes except history, she stated that she generally felt okay about her overall school experience, "Like I say, it wasn't that I didn't like school, I just needed something to keep me interested in school." She often commented on her need to have her interest held, making comments such as, "If I'm gone do something, it got to be something that's gone interest me cause if it don't interest me, I'm not gone be into it. I'm not gone do what I got to do to finish what I need to finish." And she held true to her sentiments, as she dropped out of school after completing her sophomore year.

Ironically, the only subject that held her attention in school was history. I found this interesting, as many students I have met over the years state that history is one of their least favorite subjects due to teachers' tendencies to lecture. However, Celina found history exciting.

I asked her, "Did you ever like any subjects in school?"

She replied, "Social studies, I like history."

Because I thought that was an unusual answer I asked her to expound, "What would you say was interesting about history and social studies?"

"I liked to learn about things that happened years ago. I like reading on things. Right now I still like reading on things. Like right now, they have that History Channel on cable and I watch that channel all the time," she answered.

"Yeah, I watch that too," I told her.

Celina added, "And uh, *National Geographic*, I like that too."

In spite of the fact that she did not complete her schooling, she continued to feed her love of history. She liked being transported back in time and found the ways in which people lived in the past to be absolutely interesting.

Possible Attention Deficit Disorder

Celina often commented on the need for her interest to be stimulated. In fact, the issue emerged numerous times during each interview. She addressed her inability to stay focused in school, as well as in her personal life. This deeply affected her academic performance, though she maintained that she received passing grades.

I wondered how this inability to stay focused was expressed in the classroom, "Okay, you said your favorite subject was history because you liked learning about different things, and that you are still interested in that. So when you were in school, did you do your class work while you were in school?

She replied, "Uh-huh. I didn't fail any classes or anything, I always did what I was supposed to do. I wasn't an 'A' student, but I passed with 'B's and 'C's."

So, she was able to stay on task in school, though it was difficult. "Okay, so were you ever distracted in school?"

"That's what I'm saying, my mind attention is not long. If it's something that does not interest me, I'm not gonna stay. I'm not gone do it. I know this. If it is not interesting to me, I will sit there like I'm really listening and be off in a daze," Celina answered.

"So let's talk about school in general, when you got to the point when you were bored, were you still doing your class work?" I asked, trying to get an understanding of how her wandering focus affected her in-class performance.

Celina answered matter-of-factly, "Uh-huh, I was doing it to get by."

Since "getting by" is a subjective term, I wanted to understand how she was defining it. "If you had to give yourself a grade, like A, B, C, or D, what kind of student would you say you were?"

Celina said, "A 'C' student." So she did enough work to maintain passing grades.

"What about the classes you were not interested in?" I prompted.

"I did, 'cause I knew I had to pass."

"And what grades were you getting?"

"A 'C,' I wasn't getting nothing below a C." Though she had to struggle, she had worked hard enough to pass her classes.

Because of her inability to remain focused, I thought that classes that traditionally rely heavily on lecturing would be a great challenge for her and indeed they were. "What classes were you really disinterested in?"

"English, I hate English," she said emphatically.

"Well, because I'm an English teacher, I have to know, why?" I said jokingly.

"It was something about English. I didn't like English when I was in grammar school or during the time I spent in high school. I just couldn't get off into it, but I would still pass though."

"What specifically was wrong with it?"

"Let me think. I guess it was too much reading, writing. I didn't like the reading."

"That's usually what people say," I admitted.

"I didn't like the reading." I found her reply interesting because when she told me she liked history, one of the reasons she offered was because she liked reading about the past.

"Yes, you do if you like history," I said laughing.

Celina made the distinction between the two, "That was a different story, they telling me about events and stuff like that. I can find myself getting of into that. I couldn't get off into no English. Like you know how people be reading them novels and stuff, that's a person who like to read. You won't catch me reading no novel. A big ole book, oh no. Especially if ain't nothing interesting, if it ain't about nothing. Love story, romantic story, I ain't gone be able to do it."

"Oh, you won't even read that?" I was surprised because many teenage girls find romance novels interesting; however, Celina was not one of them.

"No. It's not gone interest me. I'll sit there and read maybe about three or four pages. Somebody can say, 'Boo' and I'm distracted already and threw the book down."

Though I am not trained as a special educator, it seemed to me that Celina had Attention Deficit Disorder; however, she was never evaluated for it and did not receive special services.

One Student, Many schools

Celina attended four high schools before she dropped out after her sophomore year. In fact, she attended different types of high schools; she attended a general high school, an all-girls high school, a school specifically for pregnant girls, and an alternative high school. However, she was not retained by any of those schools and dropped out anyway. The first school she attended was a general high school and she was very fond of her experience there. Similar to other young women in the case studies, the most rewarding part of her school experience at the general high school was the extracurricular activities.

Celina described her extracurricular activities, "...in my freshman year, that's when I really liked high school 'cause I was doing things that I been interested in, that would keep me in school. Like I used to like doing ballet and modern dance and stuff like that so I took up those classes so that would keep me into school. And then I used to like working out and lifting weights and all of that and I was in the physique club at Kingston [the general high school]. So that kept my mind occupied and that kept me in school when I was going there [to Kingston] 'cause they had extracurricular activities that I enjoyed doing." Once she transferred to the all-girls high school, she started to lose interest in school because they did not offer the activities that her prior school offered.

When she expressed that she liked Kingston because of the extracurricular activities in which she was involved, I asked her, "Did you always feel like that about school? Or would you just say that your sophomore year was a good year for you? How would you compare that to your other years in school?"

Celina answered, "It was okay. It really wasn't nothing. Cause at the other school [the all-girls school] they really didn't have the activities that I had at Kingston to keep me interested in school. So, like I say if I'm gone do something, it got to be something that's gone interest me, 'cause if it don't interest me, I'm not gone be into it. I'm not gone do what I got to do, to finish what I need to finish."

Kinesthetic activities were always a motivator for Celina, as she added that they were instrumental in keeping her vested in school during her elementary years. I asked, "Did you like school when you were in elementary school?"

Celina replied, "Uh-huh. I had things to do. After school, I had cheerleading practice."

"So what you always liked about school was...," I started to say.

She answered the question before I could complete it, "...the extracurricular activities."

So the lack of activities at the all-girl high school left her with a void that was not filled. As she said repeatedly, without the physique club and the dance classes, her interest was not stimulated and she eventually found it difficult to stay motivated. As she stated, "...after I left Kingston, we moved and I started going to an all-girl school that I definitely didn't like and I stopped going for a while. That's when I messed around and got pregnant. So I didn't stay there long, I had to transfer to the maternity school."

Though Celina told me in the statement above that she dropped out because she was pregnant, she later admitted that she dropped out prior to her pregnancy.

Attendance

When I questioned Celina about her attendance, she described sporadic periods of non-attendance. There were times when she "stopped going for a while"; these periods were unofficial drop outs. Celina described the activities in which she was involved when she was not in school, "Running the street, hanging out, it wasn't nothing spectacular. You know, just hanging out. That's all, that's it. I wasn't doing nothing."

Later I asked with whom she would hang out when she decided not to attend school, and she described an older group of people who were past their high school years. "They weren't in school. Actually, the people that I hung out with, they was already out of school. I always hung out with older people, people that was like four, five years older than me—some of them did finish high school."

So hanging out with a group of older people, some of whom had not completed school, may have affected her desire to stay in school.

Cutting Classes

Though Celina told me that she did not cut class often, there were particular classes which she preferred not to attend. "Did you ever cut class?" I asked.

Celina admitted, "Yeah, I cut classes every now and then."

"What classes did you cut the most?" I questioned, as I wanted to understand how her choice of which classes to cut related to her interest in the subjects.

It was no surprise that she replied, "My English class was my first class so I would be late for her everyday. But she still passed me, you know," she said as she laughed. "That lady still passed me with a 'C' cause I would still do my work. I would make it up when we had our break, our study hall. Study hall time she would find me somewhere to make me make up my work and she still passed me."

This was interesting to me and it spoke to the character of the teacher, since she made the effort to give Celina a chance to complete her work even though she flagrantly cut her class. Because it seemed to me that Celina had Attention Deficit Disorder, I thought that the English teacher's pedagogical style might have further distanced her. "What kind of activities did you do in the class? Did she lecture?"

"She did lectures, stood up and talked sometimes and then you have to dictate, take notes and you know it just didn't interest me. I know how I am and I know how my mind span is. If it don't interest me and I can't pick up on it, I'm not gone do it," Celina emphasized once again.

So the use of the lecture format was extremely boring to Celina and it made it difficult for her to stay focused. As a result, she chose to cut English. Celina was usually arrived late to school, after her first-period English class had ended. She also cut classes at the end of the day. "When did you cut school, 'cause sometimes you said you'd leave after sixth period?"

"Well, naw, we had open campus. So sixth period, seventh period my lunch so I would go get me something to eat and would come back to eighth period 'cause that was my modern dance period. And then after that, I had another study-hall period in ninth period and then after ninth period, I had practice for body-building. I had my physique class so I would just go from modern dance to my physique class. That kept me into something 'cause it was something I liked doing," she said.

So she was selective about cutting classes and her commitment to her kinesthetic classes was evident, as she would return to school, after cutting a class, to attend those classes.

"When you got to the point when you were cutting school, when were you cutting and why?" I asked.

Celina responded, "I got pregnant and started cutting." However, this was not entirely true because earlier she mentioned that she stopped going to schools for periods of time before she was pregnant. In fact, she told me that she conceived during one of the periods when she was not attending school. Though she was officially enrolled at the all-girls school at the time, she did not return to that school.

Instead, Celina enrolled at a maternity high school. This school provided special services for expectant young mothers, and its sole focus was retaining these girls in the school system. However, once she delivered her son, she transferred to an alternative high school. She dropped out of that school as well. Though new motherhood created a strain on her completing school, Celina had the support she needed to go to school, as her maternal aunt offered to provide her with child care. Even with this support, she could not complete the alternative school.

Celina described her experience, "Yeah, I transferred and went there. After I had my son and everything, I just didn't go back to school. I tried 'cause I moved back out west with my auntie, well to my grandmother's house, because my auntie ran a day care. So that was somebody who could watch my son. That was my mother's sister. So she [her aunt] was like, 'She can move over here until she finish school, that way she can have somebody to watch the baby and she ain't got to worry about no babysitter.' So I tried that and I was gonna go to an alternative school and what happened was I had to go into the hospital for three days. I didn't know you could only miss three days. When I came back the fourth day, they told me I couldn't re-enroll; they kicked me out. So I just didn't ever go back to school."

Lack of Supervision

Both of Celina's parents worked. In fact, her mother worked full-time and attended college at night. As a result, she lacked supervision. By the time her mother noticed she was not attending school, she had missed a month. I questioned her about her lack of parental attention, "When you started cutting school and classes, where were your parents?"

"They was at work," she answered.

"They didn't get the school's call?" I asked because most schools call the parents to notify them of absences.

"They did the call. Ain't nothing they could say, if they made the call, I erased the answering machine when I got home," she stated matter-of-factly.

"So they never called them at work?" I asked.

"Uh-uh. I ain't never give them no work number. On the emergency card, I put the same number, the house number. They ain't got no work number, I don't know it," is what she told the school.

Celina, like many other high school students, discovered a way to conceal the fact that she was not attending school. Sometimes, it takes parents a while before they notice that something is wrong.

"So when did they find out?" I asked.

"My mother didn't even know, 'cause I had get kicked of school. She didn't even know but how she found out is my auntie got mad at me and told on me. They called my granddaddy's house. She thought I was going to school everyday. And my father knew and he was like, 'Whatever you wanna do'. He wasn't gone tell on me for nothing. I'm gone let you do what you want to do, that's up to you'."

It was becoming clear to me that Celina was able to evade her mother for quite a while, "So had you dropped out by that time?"

"I was out of school then. I was out about a month. But I say my father knew, but my momma didn't know. After she found out, she was still giving me whippings then. I got disciplined for it, but it didn't make me go back though. They tried to make me go back, but I didn't want to go. She would leave me bus fare and everything to get to school. I [would] leave out the door 'cause I know she gone call and I didn't know if she had the lady next door watching me to see if I left. See if I left out the door to go to school. So I would leave and go to my friend's house down the street, stay down there to about...she [Celina's mother] knew I was going to an alternative [school] so I'd be home about one o'clock or one-thirty. I'd come home at about one-thirty like I done been to school and everything and when I hear her come in the door. I would sit right there at the picnic table and act like I was doing homework. One day she didn't go to work and I ain't know she was in her room and I'm messing around and it was like 10 o'clock and she was like, 'Girl, what you doing here, you supposed to be gone to school.' And I just went ahead and told her, 'Ma, I ain't been going to school, I dropped out of school.' [She said] 'What is wrong with you?' And I answered, "Nothing".

As a result of her busy work schedule and Celina's cleverness, Celina's mother was unaware that she had not attended school for a month. This lack of supervision provided her the time to get involved in many things that led to her leaving school and getting involved in delinquent activities. Celina often talked about her need for her mother's attention, and she attributes a lot of the negative events that transpired in her life to her mother's failure to dedicate time to her.

Ms. Hurston

Celina's eighth-grade teacher went beyond the call for her students. She often talked about her experience in Ms. Hurston's class. However, the time that she valued most was the time that her teacher spent with her and other female classmates outside of school. Ms. Hurston had the girls over to her house on some weekends and they began to consider her as a mother. Celina appreciated that relationship and says that it had a great impact on her.

"Ms. Hurston, that was my favorite teacher, my eighth-grade teacher. She was a real likable lady. She felt like she really wanted to be there for the kids. You know, especially for the kids that didn't have much or whatever. Like the girls, she used to invite us over to her house and she used to give us little pajama parties. And you know she used to tell us, 'Y'all can't talk to y'all parents about things, y'all can always come to me and talk to me and we'll try to figure something out, you know, a better solution.' And she was just there for me some of the times when I needed somebody shoulder to lean on. She treated us as kids, you know. She didn't disrespect us in no type of way and we didn't disrespect her in no type of way. But she looked on it as a teacher and student relationship, as some of the girls' advisor, you know. You know the girls who stayed the weekend at her house, you know with our parents' permission. And like I say, she gave us advice when we needed it. I felt real close to her because we had a chance to open up, all the girls had a chance to open up to her without feeling ashamed or embarrassed."

"What kind of things did you used to talk about?" I asked.

"We used to talk about sex and stuff and she wanted to talk to us like she was our mother or our big sister or something. You know that's how she referred to us when we stayed at her house. [She would say] 'I'm just your big sister and y'all can talk to me about anything. If it's situations I can help y'all out in, I will to the best of my ability'. And that's how it was; the type of relationship was like a big sister to a little sister."

The relationship that Ms. Hurston formed with Celina was important to her. In fact, she told me that she still visits her at school occasionally, "I go up to the school every now and then and she still work up there at the same grammar school I went to." However, Celina has not told her that she is working as a prostitute, and that may be due to the fact that Ms. Hurston often talked to the girls about growing up to be something positive. Celina told me about Ms. Hurston's hopes for her students, "Y'all ought to finish high school and you know go to school, become a teacher," is what Ms. Hurston would tell them. Celina said that she often gave the students "encouraging words."

Celina had a very unique relationship with Ms. Hurston, and due to that relationship she performed well academically and socially, as she never cut school when she was in her classroom. She never formed that type of relationship with another teacher. She explained that to me as I tried to assess her experience with her other teachers, "Now you talk about one particular teacher being encouraging, Ms. Hurston. Would you say your other teachers made you feel like education and school was important?"

"I mean they did what teachers are supposed to do. I mean I ain't never really try to even, you know get close to them. It was just something about Ms. Hurston that I felt confident with her. You know how you get a feeling, a vibe from certain people and that's the kind of vibe I got from her. My other teachers come in, [they would say] 'Good morning, good morning,' they teach they lesson and school over with," she explained, suggesting that the other teachers were not as vested in the students as Ms. Hurston.

Because Celina thrived as a student in Ms. Hurston's class, I wanted to know if she thought having similar teachers in high school would have affected her decision to drop out. "If you had had teachers like that, let's say in high school, how do you think that would have affected you?"

"It may have helped me out a little bit more. It may have made me go in a different direction. I don't know, it may and it may not," she answered.

"But it's possible that maybe that would have made you stay?"

"It's possible."

Transition into Prostitution :"I Didn't Know He Was a Pimp for a Long Time"

Celina's transition into prostitution was gradual. Before she met the man who became and remains her pimp, she was selling drugs with her godsister; he was one of their clients. She had known him for quite a while before it even occurred to her that he was pimping women.

She described her first encounters with him, "I was working for my godsister and that's when I started selling heroin. And the guy who used to come and buy heroin from her was a pimp and me and him got to talking. I didn't know he was no pimp for a long time and I used to go out with him and he would come take me out stepping [dancing] and stuff and one day we went over to his house. I asked him, 'What's all these pictures, I know you ain't pimping?' And he talkin' about, 'Yeah, that's what I do.' I said, 'Oh my god, what the hell I done got myself into?' And so after that I had really started liking him so I had called him and asked him. I told him I wanted to see what was to it and if I ain't like it could I leave? And he was like, 'Yeah, it ain't by force, it's by choice.' And I tried it and been there since."

The first time he asked her to work for him, she did not believe him and did not start immediately. He began to persuade her by reinforcing that she had a choice and was free to leave at anytime. She described his offer to her, "He had asked me but I told him, 'Stop playing with me. You know, I'm not into that. I can't see myself standing on no corner, "hoeing" for nobody and woo, woo, woo.' He said alright and he left it at that. And so me with my curious, curious butt, I'm like, 'Let's see what's to this.' And like I say, he say, 'If you ain't like it, I ain't forcing you to be here, you can leave at anytime.' I tried it for that week and seen how much money I can get and I was like, "I can do this."

Because she seemed to be highly motivated by the money, I wanted to clarify how much she was earning, "How much money did you make?"

"The first night I worked I think I was out there for like two hours and I got like three-hundred-something dollars. I'm like, "man." I had two dates [sexual encounters] 'cause one was a hotel date and I had charged him $150. And then they gave me like a $25 tip or whatever. And once I got to meet some of the girls out there and they start showing me where to park at and what to charge a trick. And like by the weekend, I was checking like $700 to $800 a night. And I'm like, 'I can do this. I can do this.'" Though she was giving all of her money to her pimp, the money caused her to continue to work the streets.

Celina's transition into prostitution had more to do with her feelings about the man who introduced her to it and her own curiosity than any need, due to the fact that she was making money from drug sells. As she often told me during our talks, her mother gave her everything as a child and as an adult. She took care of her son when Celina gave birth to him, and he now lives with her, visiting Celina on the weekends. Therefore, she had a great deal of financial support from her mother and did not need the money she earned from prostitution. She needed the attention that her pimp offered her and still needs it today, as she told me she thought she would be with him forever. Selling and using drugs was a part of Celina's lifestyle as well as Carmella's. As a reformed prostitute told me, drug usage and prostitution are coupled together, and a continuous cycle for many young women in the industry; they find themselves using drugs to cope with the stress and depression of prostitution, but the drugs increase their need to make money through prostitution. She explained that once this cycle ensues, it is extremely difficult to break. However, Celina told me that she was never in that cycle; she used drugs recreationally and was not dependent. She sold drugs prior to prostituting, but had not since she started working the streets, though she used them occasionally.

Working the Streets

Celina has worked the streets for years, traveling the country with the same pimp. She has tried various forms of prostitution. "I do it all. I had my own service. I done had my own service since I been working the streets. I done been across the country working the streets, I went from New York to Hawaii, Canada, Texas," she said.

"Dallas, Harry Hines Boulevard?" I asked her, referring to a popular street known for prostitution. Ironically, this was the area I was patrolling the night I accompanied a police officer, meeting those school-age girls that night prompted me to do this study.

"Harry Hines Road," she confirmed.

"I met some girls out there," I shared with her and we began to talk about how prostitution is different in that area. "It's a different thing down there, girls drive around in cars." I was referring to the fact that many street prostitutes do not stand on the corner to solicit clients. They actually drive down the boulevard in revealing clothes with the interior light on as a signal that they are looking for clients.

"Yeah," she agreed as she told me about other cities in which she has worked. "And Miami. It really ain't nowhere I haven't been. I done been to Montreal, Canada. And then, I mean you still standing on the corner. You know, well not all, like in Dallas, they riding around in the car. But here, they standing on corners. Anywhere I know I can get some money, I know a trick [a client] gone spend $200 or $300 or better. That's where I'm gone go and that's what I'm gone do."

Life with Her Pimp

As I listened to Celina describe the relationship between herself and her pimp, I could see that she had reconciled a lot of the issues that many people have with women selling their bodies and giving the money to a pimp. She minimized that aspect of prostitution and was not disturbed by it. She also discounted the physical abuse that he inflicts upon her. I asked, "Do you ever fight or does he ever beat you?"

She began to make excuses for him, "You know, he have his ways and I have mine. And yes, I ain't gone lie, he has hit me a couple of times or whatever, but now since we done got really off into the relationship or whatever, we don't argue and fight. The only time we argue and fight about something is when he feel like I been getting high 'cause he don't like me getting high."

From her response, it seemed as though she thought that the abuse was acceptable because she quickly added that she has her "ways" as well.

"So when you get high, what do you get high off of?" I asked.

"Just heroin. And he got a real bad temper so I just try to stay out his face. But other than that, we get along fine," she replied. It was evident that she did not consider heroin a serious drug. Also, she did not seem to have a problem with the fact that she had to avoid him if she did not want to be beat for using drugs.

"Do you all live together?" I asked. Celina nodded yes. "Just you and him or does anyone else live with you?

She replied, "Well, right now it's me and him and my wife-in-law [prostitute with the same pimp]. He got another girl. Yeah, until my house get ready, 'cause I just moved out my house. We was in an apartment while the house getting ready 'cause it's being built from the ground and it won't be ready until next year."

"Is that your house?" I asked, wanting to know if she had any ownership in the house she provided the finances to build.

"It's our house together," she replied. However, I did not ask her if she was listed as an owner on the house.

Celina was the only woman in the study who actually had a pimp. As she talked about her arrangements with him, it was clear to me that she had bought into the system of selling her body and giving him all of the proceeds. She explained why she did not have an issue with giving him all of her money, "I always gave him all the money. It's like I know where my money going. He don't get high, he drink on the weekends or whatever, but he don't get high and I know where every dime going. Every dime, car note, you know, mortgage. You know, things we like to do or whatever. I know where all the money going so it wasn't no big thing about, why you give him all your money. I know where that money going. It ain't like I don't see it. You know, it didn't bother me."

"So do you get what you need or want? He doesn't deny you anything?" I asked, wondering how she negotiated these things.

"Ain't nothing he don't, I'll ask him for whatever and he'll give it to me," she said emphatically.

Celina had been with this pimp for years and it is difficult to imagine that she never wanted to leave him and keep the money for herself. I recalled Carmella's attitude about not having a pimp and thought she must have thought about working for herself at some point. I asked her, "Have you ever wanted to do your own thing?"

Celina's explanation to this question clarified a lot about the rules of street prostitution as she explained, "Well, actually, where we work at and all the places you go, you can't just be out there and don't have no man. Cause it be other women out there who gone tell they man you ain't got no man and they'll try to take your money. It be other pimps and other hoes and they'll try to take your money. How I know, 'cause I done did it. It be girls out there working and ain't got no man, talking about they got a pimp. Bitch, break yourself 'cause that's the rules and regulations of the game. Like I say, it don't bother me, this what I choose to do so I knew I was gone have to give all my money to him so it really ain't no big deal. I'm used to it now."

It was clear that she thought giving the money to a pimp was the way it was supposed to be and resented women who worked the streets without a pimp, also known as "outlaws," as she thought they should "break themselves" or bow to giving their money to a man. She told her pimp about the wayward women who were working the streets alone. As a result, these women would have to "choose" a pimp or leave the area.

The Family: "I Was Living in a Dysfunctional Household"

The majority of my talks with Celina centered around her family relationship. She grew up in a two-parent household with her two older brothers. Both of her parents were employed and provided financial comfort for Celina and her brothers. She often stated that they never lacked anything. However, while the family was economically stable, they were emotionally unstable. She described frequent and brutal fights between her parents. Though she had two brothers, they were rarely home; therefore, the responsibility of breaking up the fights fell on her.

These fights had a severe impact on Celina's sense of safety. She also carried the burden of feeling as though she had to prevent or stop the fighting once it began. She described some of the brawls, "It used to bother me. What can I do? 'Cause if I try to break it up, he'll push me out the way. I have seen my father break my momma leg, break her ribs. I done seen her bust his head or whatever. You know those big old ash trays? I done seen her bust his head with that. I had went out to the club when they couldn't find nobody to watch me, 'cause it used to be a club our family owned and my daddy used to mess around on my mother a lot. And the lady that he was messing around with shot my mother in the arm. We had to rush her to County Hospital. I'll never forget none of that. Right now to this day, when I bring it up she say, 'Girl, you don't know what you talking about.' She want to keep it in the past. You know what I mean? What's the point in keeping it in the past when it's the truth? And she always say you don't know what you're talking about. Okay, I know I ain't crazy. I remember everything."

Celina's mother never addressed the physical abuse that she suffered or the emotional abuse of her children. However, Celina frequently talked about the negative effect that it had on everyone in the household. Her mother found other ways of dealing with the abuse, and the children found escape in the streets, as the brothers were always away from the house. As Celina got older, she too stayed away from home. The situation with her parents continued throughout her adolescent years, as they did not divorce until she was 18.

"She Gave Me Everything; I Didn't Want That, I Wanted Her Attention:" Celina's Mother

Though Celina's mother provided her with more material things than she needed or wanted, she did not provide her with the attention and love she needed. While Celina was growing up, her mother was always busy with work and school. She bought Celina clothes and jewelry as penance for her absence. Her mother's willingness to shower her with extravagant gifts made her angry. Celina thought that it did not compensate for her lack of attention. She deeply resented that her mother was more involved in her own life than her children's. I inquired about her mother's activities when she was away from home and surprisingly, she spent very little time socializing. Instead, she was working full-time and attending night classes in pursuit of her college degree. Though these things were meant to help her provide for her family, Celina didn't see it that way. She saw her mother as self-absorbed. "She was at school. She would work insurance during the day time and at night she was going to school. So I was just, you know, my father was there. He would come home from work and make sure I'm okay and cool and everything and make me something to eat. Eventually, in the end, he'd leave and tell me he'd be back and whatever and I'd be okay." As a result, Celina spent a lot of time alone or hanging out with friends.

Celina's relationship with her mother continues to be riddled with conflict, verbal confrontation, and verbal abuse. She described their relationship, "We ain't have no relationship. It was 'do this' and 'do that.' And that was all, that's it. [She would say] 'I don't want no back talk.' We didn't have no relationship. Now since I done got older, we have a relationship now. I'm not gone say it's the most perfect relationship, but it's way better than it used to be. You know, 'cause like I say, I'm older now and I can say how I feel. 'Cause I used to be scared of her when I was a child, you know, 'cause I couldn't say how I felt. It was always, 'You gone do this and that's all I said and ain't no back talk or none of that.' And that wasn't just towards me, it was towards my brothers n'em too. So, when I got older, I was able to say what I wanted to say, when I wanted to say it."

Due to the fact that the household was unstable because of the fighting and lack of supervision, it was important for Celina to talk with her mother about some of these issues. However, her mother was in denial about what happened; she still does not talk to Celina about the problems in the house. Celina resented having to deal with those emotions on her own.

"I resented it 'cause it's a lot of things, emotional feelings that I was going through that I think I should have been able to talk to my mother about and I couldn't talk to her about it. You know, it bothered me. You know, emotionally, physically, and everything; mentally and everything, up until right now today. I'm not blaming her for the things that, for the situation that I'm in or whatever, but she got a lot to do with it."

Some of the things that she should have been able to share with her mother and did not were her pregnancy and the molestation by her mother's brother. Instead, she shared her pregnancy with her father first and told her mother when she could no longer hide her bulging stomach. Even today, no one knows about the molestation.

"Tell me about what kind of person your mother is," I asked, and Celina started to chuckle.

"Arrogant. She's very arrogant. She's a sweet person to a certain extent. I love her to death," she said and I was surprised because we had many conversations before and she never told me that she loved her mother. Instead, she always had a hint of anger in her voice each time she talked about her. This time, she was trying to be more objective. "...I never wish nothing bad will happen to her 'cause I don't know what I'll do without her. But, she have her ways, she just set in her own ways and can't nobody change her. So she's very arrogant and she's very bossy. She think everybody suppose to do for her and, 'Momma, we grown. We ain't got to do nothing for you. Don't nobody have to do, we do it because you our momma,'" she said, role-playing as she often did.

"Like a couple weeks ago, my guy was saying, 'You starting to act just like your momma, miserable.' She seems like she's miserable, you know. She ain't got no man, all she do is sit in the house and drink. I told her, 'You gone drink your life away.' Well now she done started back to working again and now she just drink on the weekend, but it's like she miserable," she said, shaking her head.

One of the reasons that Celina thought that her mother was miserable was because she didn't have a man. She did not seem to consider all the abuse her mother had suffered from her father, and how those experiences may have led to her desire to be alone. Her mother had found an escape through alcohol, and Celina described her drinking as quite a problem.

I asked her, "Would you say she's an alcoholic?"

To which she replied, "Naw, she just like to drink." I found her answer interesting because what she described definitely sounded like alcoholism to me.

"On the weekend she drinks, but like I say she just started working at the office a month ago so she don't drink, every now and then. When she didn't have nothing to do, she drank all week long. After she had left the other job, she'd drink everyday. I'll call and I'll know in her voice when she sounded sober. 'Ma, you drinking again?' [She would say] 'I could do what I want to do.' And I said, 'I ain't say you can't do what you want to do in your house, I just asked if you been drinking again.' My older brother was like, 'you need to call and talk to momma cause she drinking everyday.' And I'm like, 'Well, okay I'll come over there and talk to her. And like I told him, 'Well momma, that's her way of relaxing, she worked hard for it,' she said, making excuses for her excessive drinking.

However, she did talk to her mother about it. [I told her], "Momma, you can't be drinking like this everyday.' You know, I say, 'I don't want you to leave. If you leave I want it to be of natural causes, not cause of sclerosis of the liver.' You know, but she has slowed up a lot. It be some weekends like if I call over there, 'cause my son don't come over for the weekend and I be like, 'What mamma doing?' He would say, 'She's sleep.' I ask, 'Is she sleep 'cause she been drinking,' and he say, 'She only drank a little bit.' He told me she don't be drinking like she used to. She'll get like a pint or something and you know. It ain't gone be no fifth. So, I'll call and she'll call me back when she get up or something. She kinda, she set in her ways. And can't nobody change her. I love her to death. She always gone be my mother. You only have one."

The fact that she said that she was not drinking the way she used to, saying that she only consumes a pint of liquor a day, was alarming. As she explained, there was a point at which she was drinking a fifth of liquor a day. Even with this excessive drinking and her virtually passing out, Celina still did not consider her mother an alcoholic.

While in her drunken state, she sometimes calls Celina and verbally assaults her as she often did while Celina was a child, "I feel bad sometimes and think about the things she say, cruel, I'm talking abut real, real cruel and sometimes she get drunk and I don't know what it is. She just drink, you drink enough and then you think about your past and the things that done happen to you. She would get drunk and call me and just cuss me out and I'll be like, 'What, is it because of my daddy?' She would call and be like, 'You dirty bitch and whore.' And I be like, 'What I do?' And you know she would do that when I was younger though, she'd call me all type of Black bitches for nothing. You know I used to always wonder about that stuff, but now when she do it I be like, 'Okay, whatever,' and just hang the phone up."

Celina does not attribute her mother's anger and name calling to her prostitution, though she admits that her mother disapproves of it, "At first she reacted like any other normal mother, they not gone want to see they child on no street and especially working and giving all her money to a man...but now she done got pass it...She told me, I don't like what y'all do. Like she told him [her pimp], it's not that I don't like you, but I don't like what you do. Like I say, now she don't even bother. It's been so long she like, 'She gone do what she want to do no matter how I preach to her, she'll come to her senses one day."

Though Celina loves her mother, her relationship with her remains tumultuous and verbally abusive at times. Sometimes she cries after their confrontations. It is an open wound that has never healed.

"My Father, That's My Heart:" Celina's Relationship with Her Father

Celina was very close to her father while she was growing up, and she is close to him still. As she told me, "My father, now that's my heart. That's my pride and joy. Whatever, he gave me the attention that my mother didn't give me. He was there for me. Anytime I needed my daddy, he was there for me. I don't have no complaints about my daddy. Right now today, I can call him crying or whatever and he gone come see about his baby."

Though he and her mother had an abusive relationship, she never addressed how she felt about her father being physically violent towards her mother. It seems as though her parent's marriage has not affected the way she feels about him. Maybe her willingness to overlook the abuse is based on the fact that he was always supportive of her. He has been her emotional support for years. As a result, he has seen her through many difficult times. When Celina found out she was pregnant, she told him first; he knew about it during her first month of pregnancy. She described him as supportive, "My father was like, 'Whatever you wanna do, that's what we gone do'. So my daddy was like, 'I tell you what, I'll get the money up to get you an abortion' and I'm like, 'Okay, cool."   However, Celina kept her son because the child's father pleaded with her to have the baby. Though she was still planning to have an abortion, she did not because the child's father was killed before she had the operation and the tragedy persuaded her to continue the pregnancy. Again, her father was her primary emotional support as she advanced in her pregnancy and coped with the death of her son's father.

Celina's father knows that she is a prostitute, but she said that he supports her in spite on this. I asked her, "Tell me what your relationship with your father was like before you started prostituting and what does he think about it now?"

Celina maintained, "It hasn't changed. It's been the same always. It's been the same and even when I told him and everything, my father never acted different towards me 'cause me and him have always had the type of relationship where I could go to my daddy and talk to him about anything. I could tell my dad and he gone work out something...me and my daddy's relationship hasn't changed and I hope it don't never change."

Like her mother, he father disapproves of her lifestyle; however, he does not give the verbal backlash that her mother does, "He critical about the prostitution. I told him [about the prostitution]; I don't hide nothing from him. Like he say, he don't like it but that's what I wanna do and it's not gone stop. I'm his daughter and I'll always be his daughter. Him and my guy [her pimp] get along fine and everything."

Her Son

Celina's son lives with her mother; however, he visits her on the weekend. She is very proud of her son and maintains that she is very concerned about his education. She wants him to stay in school and avoid some of the mistakes that she has made. Because she is concerned about him being exposed to the wrong influences, he attends a Catholic school. She felt that the environment would be safer and that he would be able to maintain his focus.

Celina has a very close relationship with her son, in spite of the fact that he does not live with her. She says that they talk about everything and that she does not keep anything from him, "...I talk to him about everything 'cause I don't want me and him to have the type of relationship me and her had. So, me and him talk about everything. I talk to him about the little girls and I'm saying is he ready to have sex, we talk about condoms, we talk about everything. Everything I think that he needs to know about me and I need to know about him, I'm gone bring the conversation up and if I don't, he will. 'Cause I told him you ain't got to lie to me about nothing. We not hiding nothing from each other."

Though she said that she does not hide anything from him, that is not entirely true because she has not told him that she is a prostitute. Once he inquired about the manner in which she dresses, and she did not tell him the truth, "I told him I dance at a club. I told him that 'cause he be there on the weekend. Well, now, when he was coming up, I used to go out the house with my gear on but as he got a little older, I start throwing on jogging suits and just change my clothes in the car. Then he asked me one day, '...Ma, why you got to have that little ole miniskirt on? Where going with those boots on?' You know if I have boots on and I say, 'Boy, shut up and get out my business.' So I just told him I dance at a club. He say, 'You like that?' I say, 'I'm just paying the bills.' He said okay. I say, 'You don't want me to dance at no club?' He go, 'Mamma, I can't tell you what to do."

So she conceals her prostitution from him, though she says that she will tell him the truth when he gets older, "I told my guy when he get older then I'm gone tell him about the prostitution thing. Right now I don't think he's ready for that, I feel like I'm lying to him."

The Psychological: "I Try Not To Let Things Bother Me"

Celina's coping mechanism for the tragedies that she has suffered in life is to mentally "block them out" of her mind. She never seemed to connect her prostitution with her life events. The only connection that she made is the treatment she received from her mother. Though she says she is not blaming her mother, she was a factor in her decision to prostitute. One of the tragedies that she never addressed was the molestation.

Molestation

When Celina was seven years old, she was molested and never shared it with anyone, "I was molested as a child by my mother's brother and right to this day she doesn't know and he [her father] don't know. I never confronted him or told anybody about it in the family because that's my mother's favorite brother and I didn't want them to stop talking."

This was her first encounter with sex and it must have traumatized her, yet she did not tell anyone. She described her reaction, "It didn't bother me because I had kind of kept it in the back of my mind for so long. I think as I got older, that's when it started bothering me, 'cause I ain't really think about it. I thought about it and it would come and go and I would just move on. But by me starting to work on things, a lot of feelings is starting to come out pertaining to how I grew up and how I was raised. But it's okay with me to a certain extent. I try not to let things bother me too much."

Neglect and Verbal Abuse from her Mother

Celina's relationship with her mother has been one that has inflicted a great deal of hurt; however, she has just begun to deflect her mother's verbal attacks. As she stated, when her mother begins to insult her, she hangs up the phone. Though she will withdraw from the conflict, it remains a problem because she talks to her daily and the attacks may start at anytime. She has never told her mother how she feels about her not being there for her when she was growing up or about the things she says to her, though she is deeply affected by it.

Violence in the Household

Though her father and mother fought frequently, she does not seem to address his part in the fights. However, she does not like the fact that her mother will not address the violence. She wanted to talk with her mother about the fighting, but she denies them or avoids the topic. Celina never mentioned discussing the fights with her father. However, she was terrified by their fighting and carried the burden of having to break up the fights. Yet, she never received counseling for the trauma.

The Future: "I Ain't Gone Give Up"

"I Still Got Time, I Ain't Gone Give Up
on What I Always Wanted to Do."

Celina avoided making plans for the future. She told me that every time she made plans, she was unable to follow through with them. As a result, she was hesitant to plan. This is an issue because her inability to follow-through with plans has prevented her from going back to school to get a G.E.D. or to follow her dreams of owning her own beauty shop. In fact, she made plans to work with me on G.E.D. preparation and never followed through. Though she has not returned to school, she values education for herself and her son.

"If I could change back the hands of time, I would still be in school right now, today," Celina said.

"So if you would have stayed in school, what do you think you would have done?" I asked, wanting to know her aspirations for the future.

Indeed, she had hopes, "If I had stayed in school and did the things I had planned on doing, as I got grown I had planned on finishing school, going to beauty school, getting my own license, getting my own beauty shop. I'd be in my beauty shop right about now. If I would have did the things, that's what I wanted to do as I got older."

"Okay, well you kind of did that somewhat because you started school [beauty school]. So what happened to make you leave beauty school?"

"I met the guy I'm with now, my man [her pimp]. But he always telling me, I need to go back, I need to go back. That you still need something to fall on, stuff like that. I just ain't went back," she answered.

"You said you need something to fall back on. So, as far as your long term plans, do you have any? Like what are you going to do five years from now?" I asked with pause, knowing she rarely made plans.

"I had thought about it, but I ain't made no total long-term plans 'cause I don't know what God may have in store for me 'cause I don't like making plans 'cause every time I do, I don't follow through. I just go with the flow and do day by day," she said again as she had so many times before.

I continued to prompt her to think about the future, "If you didn't have to plan it, let's just say, if you could say where you would like to be in five years or what you'd be doing, what would you do?"

"I still want my own beauty shop. I'd go get my license for hair and do hair. I mean that's something that would keep my mind occupied, that's what I like to do." She was committed to the idea of owning her own shop.

"So if you had a beauty shop and everything was up and running well, do you think you still might be working the streets?" I questioned, wondering if there was any way that she would stop prostituting.

"Uh-uh," she said indicating no. "I wouldn't have time 'cause my mind would be dedicated to that and that only."

"When you start your own shop, that's all you would do? You wouldn't work anymore on the street?" I asked to clarify.

"I mean I may have some regular clients, but as far as me standing out there, naw, I wouldn't." So, even if she had other income, she would still prostitute to some degree. "I ain't gone give up. I still got time. I ain't gone give up on what I always wanted to do."

"And eventually one day can you see yourself doing that [owning a shop] and that only?"

"Uh-huh, she answered, indicating yes.

Understanding Celina: An Interpretation

Emotional Motivations for Prostitution

Though Celina grew up in a community that was both impoverished and crime-ridden, her family was financially stable. Both of her parents were gainfully employed and provided her with all of the necessities and many of her wants. As she told me on more than one occasion, her mother showered her with gifts such as jewelry and clothes. Celina viewed the amount of material things she received as excessive, stating that she did not need all of those things and that they were not a replacement for her mother's love and attention. She described a household that was financially sound, but "dysfunctional" where her parents fought on a constant basis, sometimes to the point where one of them would have to be hospitalized. She described a mother who was so emotionally distant that she was afraid to tell her about being molested by her favorite brother. Though she had brothers, she was often left alone to referee her parents' fights. These things seem to have left an emotional void in Celina, one that she filled with the attention of a pimp. Therefore, Celina is a part of the small percentage (18% is the highest percentage found per literature review) of young women who enter prostitution for emotional rather than financial reasons (Silbert & Pines, 1982).

Her basis for entering prostitution for emotional reasons is supported by the fact that she was dealing drugs when she met her pimp. Though selling drugs is illegal, it is lucrative and she did not need the money that prostitution provided. In fact, the money she made from dealing was her own and did not have to be relinquished to a pimp. However, she was drawn into street prostitution out of what she calls "curiosity," though that interest only emerged after she had been dating the pimp and had grown to "like" him. It is true that some women enter prostitution for a sense of adventure[15], (Ivers & Carlson, 1987; Caplan, 1984; Schaffer & DeBlassie, 1984), though I do not believe it was Celina's primary reason. My assertion is based on her views of pimping and prostitution prior to her personal relationship with him; she thought the fact that he was a pimp was ridiculous. After dating him, she was willing to try it, not because he forced her but because she wanted to do whatever it took to keep his "love" and attention as do some prostitutes (Silbert & Pines, 1982).

In a study of adolescent prostitutes' psychological motivations for entering prostitution, MacVicar and Dillon (1980) found

> ...these women to be emotionally deprived. The defense mechanisms utilized by the women, splitting, projection, idealization, stemmed from impoverished and inadequate parental relationships, especially with their mothers....Their entry into prostitution came soon after encountering a pimp, at a time when they were threatened with the loss of an important love object, (the mother or a lover/spouse). Not being able to tolerate separation or feelings of emptiness or desperation, they formed a relationship with the pimp. This relationship was characterized by masochistic submission to an idealized object, manifesting a transferal to the pimp of longings for a union with the all-good mother. (pp. 148, 153)

Though Celina described a close relationship with her father, she was emotionally deprived and verbally abused by her mother. Also, Celina began prostituting a year or so after the death of her son's father, which would address the loss of an important love relationship. Her willingness to stay with her pimp and attribute his physical abuse to concern and caring about her drug usage can be viewed as an desire to view the relationship as a parental one.

"Bitch, You Better Break Yourself:" Castigation
of Independent Prostitutes

When Celina first became a prostitute, she admits that she had to adjust to giving her pimp all of the money. However, she now gives him the money without hesitation. She attributed her willingness to give him the money to her knowledge of how the funds are spent. She also maintained that he supplies all of her needs and wants. The fact that she has to ask him to provide her every need is not a problem and she does not give consideration to the parent/child-like nature of such an arrangement. She is comfortable with complete reliance upon her pimp. She does not seem to realize that she is taking care of the pimp and that he's not taking care of her. This disillusion is common among adolescent prostitutes—though Celina is now an adult and still holds this view—as Weisberg states:

> According to prostitutes, the pimp also is "someone who cares about me," "Someone who provides respect," "someone who makes an economic contribution," and "someone who provides drugs." Gray agrees that adolescents feel they need a man to take care of business and to give them social status. She comments that although, paradoxically, the prostitute is the financial provider...the pimp serves as the major decision maker, authority, and controller of funds. In return the women provide him with emotional support and earn money for him. (1985, p. 105)

As a result of her willingness to give her earnings to her pimp, she expects all street prostitutes to do the same. She is vehemently against prostitutes working the streets for themselves, and has told her pimp about these wayward prostitutes. Women who work the streets without a pimp, known as "renegades" or "outlaws" (Williamson, 1999) are prey to violence and robbery by pimps and other prostitutes and are viewed as pariahs among pariahs, as they threaten to dismantle or challenge the hierarchy and social order of this subculture. Celina's sentiments towards these women were, "Bitch break yourself 'cause that's the rules and regulations of the game." She went on to explain that women can not work the streets without a man and every street prostitute must adhere to those rules. Celina is an enforcer of the rules, as she has exposed what I have termed "pimpless" prostitutes to her pimp so that he could "break" them, meaning force them to adhere by choosing to be represented by a pimp or leave the area.

The research that addresses the relationships among prostitutes suggests that there is camaraderie among them, that they tend to each other's welfare (Williamson, 1999). While this is true to a certain degree, it more true among prostitutes with the same pimp, known as wife-in-laws. Though the courtesy is extended to prostitutes who do not have the same pimp as well, it is not extended to the pimpless prostitute. That prostitute is castigated by those who have pimps as if to ask, "Who does she think she is to work the streets without a man?" Therefore, a street prostitute must "break" herself or submit to a pimp by going through the rites of passage of "choosing" a pimp. If she does not, the consequences are brutal, as other street prostitutes police the pimpless prostitutes. In this sense, the oppressed (meaning street prostitutes with pimps) become the oppressors as they eagerly patrol and await the "breaking" or ritualized oppression of the pimpless prostitute. This form of oppression is a clear example of Freire's theory of the oppressed; as he states, "...the oppressed, instead of striving for liberation, tend themselves to become oppressors, or 'sub-oppressors'" (Freire, 1998, p. 27).

Celina's level of social consciousness did not allow her to realize that the oppression of the pimpless prostitute is an oppression of herself, though such pondering of male and female power relationships never seemed to occur to her. During the times that I talked with her, she never mentioned anything indicating that she thought about the empowerment of women. She seemed to be unaware of the fact that as a woman, she was being exploited by a man by selling her body for his benefit. Her understanding of male/female power relationships was that women should be subject to men, as she abides and thinks that other prostitutes should abide by the "rules and regulations of the game." Also, that women without men lack value and lead less fulfilling lives, as she stated, "She [her mother] seems like she's miserable you know, she ain't got no man..." Therefore, for Celina a woman's value and happiness is directly related to her relationship with a man.

Failure to Be Tracked or Referred for Special Education Services

Celina often mentioned that she had difficultly paying attention in class and that her mind would wander. She posited that staying focus remains a problem for her today. After the interviews, it was evident to me that she had Attention Deficit Disorder; however, she was never referred to special education services for an evaluation.

Celina admitted that she did enough work in class to "get by"; she was a "C" student and was well-behaved. She never gave the teachers any problems. Because of Celina's "good" behavior and satisfactory academic record, she was undetected by the teacher. Her teachers did not engage her in active learning, as she was able to, "...sit there like I'm really listening and be off in a daze." This phenomenon of fading into the background of the classroom and becoming "invisible" is one way in which girls are marginalized in the classroom, as girls have historically been socialized to be less aggressive and socially agreeable (Henry, 1998; Omolade, 1994; Sadker & Sadker, 1994). Since girls receive less pedagogical attention in class, girls in need of special attention and services, like Celina, are further marginalized (Horgan, 1995; Sadker & Sadker, 1994; Yates 1993). Since Celina's disability was not a behaviorally based one (i.e., Behavior Disorder, Hyperactivity Disorder), she faded away into silence, unrecognized by her teachers.

CHAPTER SEVEN

Voyage to Buddha: "I Needed Some Place to Stay"

Buddha sat in the coffee shop bobbing her head to the music playing through her headphones. She had her eyes closed and it seemed as though she had been transported to a place far away. She was listening to the *Voyage to India* CD voiced by the soulful sounds of India.Arie, a young African American female vocalist. India.Arie was her favorite artist largely due to her lyrics, which often address self-esteem issues and overcoming obstacles. Buddha described her lyrics as healing and soothing. The particular song she was listening to was "Get It Together," which deals with the subject of sexual abuse and emotional recovery. The chorus encourages the listener to, "Get it together/You wanna heal your body/You have to heal your heart/Whatsoever is so you will reap/Get it together/You can fly fly." As I listened to the story of Buddha's life and the music of India.Arie, I realized that the songs were cathartic for her; they helped her to make sense of a world that had been unkind. I often think one of the reasons that Buddha was so willing to share her story was because she was working through a lot of her life experiences at the time. Though she was only 18 years old, she had experienced a great deal of adversity. In spite of it all, she sat across from me, smiling and willing to share the first chapters of her life.

"Tell me about yourself, things like who you are, where you grew up." Buddha began to share her life story with me. She grew up on the south side of Chicago in an area that holds great significance for both the city's history and African American history. The area is known as Bronzeville, and was home to many African Americans who migrated from the south. The area is famous for the cultural contributions that were made to the arts such as blues, jazz, gospel, and literature. In the 1920s to the 1940s, Bronzeville was the cultural center of Black life in Chicago and a burgeoning neighborhood. However, the community began to crumble in the following decades, suffering drug infiltration, unemployment, and high crime rates. As a result, it became one of the poorest and most unsafe neighborhoods in the community, though today it is enjoying revitalization due to gentrification. Buddha lived in the community during the time in which crime and unemployment occured at an alarming rate. When I asked her how she would describe her community, she confirmed this by stating, "Mostly ghetto. That's all I can say, plain-out ghetto...I mean, it wasn't too good. We had people fighting over there every day. You had to deal with maybe drug dealing, women who was prostituting like out in the open."

Buddha spoke of women prostituting in the open because she was not a street prostitute. Instead, she was involved in "survival sex," meaning that she did not exchange sex for money; rather, she exchanged sex for a place to live.

Though her community was dangerous and crime-ridden, she used to feel safe until tragedy struck her family, "Well, at first, I did used to feel safe around there because everybody knew us. Till then about three years ago...that's why we first moved from around there, 'cause my auntie got killed around there." So she and her family's sense of safety were shattered, prompting them to move to another community three years ago. I asked Buddha about her idea of a safe community.

"What I would [consider a safe community is] where you can let your kids ride bikes. You ain't got to worry about no bullet hitting them or something. Like the community I stay in right now. You ain't got to worry about nobody shooting one of your babies, your baby boy on the street, you ain't got to worry about that here. That's a lot 'cause people, you know, don't nobody sell drugs around there where we stay at," she said. So her family was able to leave

Bronzeville, which is suffering from high crime rates, though that is beginning to change.

Buddha was raised by her paternal grandmother and lived in their house with her sisters, aunts, uncles, and cousins. In short, she lived in a crowded household. Though there were many adults in her household, Buddha lacked supervision and attention. In fact, she was able to conceal her pregnancy for nine months before anyone knew that she was pregnant. The lack of supervision also enabled her to cut school and hang out with her friends. Buddha is still affected by the lack of parental guidance and support; "[The] only thing that I could say was the worst thing and that was just my parents not being around. That's the only thing that really affected me growing up and I'm still having problems with it."

Though Buddha said that she liked school, she was constantly involved in fights and was suspended at times, "Before I was pregnant, it was like every other day I was in fights. I was suspended about four or five times, but I fought more than that." In spite of the fights, Buddha maintained that she liked school. The social challenges did not outweigh her appreciation of her schooling experience. She liked school though she could not really articulate why, "Well, I liked it. We wasn't really doing much at our school. I liked it there. It was cool." After listening to all of the interviews, I realized that she enjoyed both the relationships she had formed with her teachers as well as the reading she did for school.

Buddha dropped out of school in the eighth grade because she was pregnant with her son. However, she attended school until her ninth month, though she was sick. Eventually, she was too ill to attend and stopped going to school. Though many adults lived in her house, they all worked or attended school as well, so she did not have anyone to care for her son during the day. As a result, she was unable to return to school; she told me, "I didn't graduate. I ditched school 'cause I was like having problems in that school, like fighting every day. Really wasn't paying attention in classroom so I never did graduate from the eighth grade. But I was doing okay in school so they put me in the ninth grade. The school closed down, so after that I just didn't go back to school, never got a diploma from eighth grade or high school."

She was 14 years old when she had her baby and dropped out, and never completed the eighth grade. She sought jobs but was unable to secure one due to her lack of education. So when she got into a conflict with her grandmother and was asked to leave the house, uneducated and unemployed, she found herself living with a man, trading sex for shelter.

Dropping Out: "I Didn't Finish School Because I Had a Baby Young"

The Love of Reading

Buddha admitted that she was not a stellar student. In fact, she was a little below average, "I was like a so-so student...'C' and 'D' student. I know I didn't have 'F's...never had a 'F', but 'C's and 'D's.

Her mediocre grades were not an indication of how she felt about school, as she described really enjoying school. I asked her, "Was there ever a time when you did not like school?"

She replied, "No, I liked it—I don't know. I just liked being in school then, I used to do all my work in school. I get bad grades or whatever, but I liked school."

I tried to encourage Buddha to elaborate on what she liked about school, and she began to tell me about her favorite subjects. Of all of the four participants, Buddha was the first to respond, "Reading."

"What kind of things did you like to read?" I asked.

She responded, "Novels, like books and stuff. And in Social Studies...I raised my hand to read. I was like reading anything."

Her love of reading and language arts was evident, as she loved reading and writing poetry. Once I asked, "What do you feel you do well, something you're good at?"

To which she replied, "Writing poems."

"What kind of stuff do you write about?" I questioned.

"Love. I write just what I feel about anything," Buddha explained.

"Do you read poetry?"

"Uh-huh, my favorite poet is...Michael Reese, I love his poems, all of them. I love his poems. And Maya Angelou," she added with excitement in her voice.

Buddha explained that she had been introduced to poetry by one of her English teachers and had been interested in it ever since. She often wrote poems and kept them in a journal. As she stated, she would write about whatever she was feeling. Her love of poetry probably accounts for her affinity for the vocalist India.Arie, as her lyrics are poetic in nature. Buddha used poetry as a medium for expressing both positive and negative emotions. Many times her emotions would rage out of control, resulting in conflict with her peers and teachers at school.

Taunting by Peers, Fights, and Attitude:
An Undiagnosed Behavioral Disorder

Though Buddha liked school, she was a below-average student and she attributed that to the taunting she experienced from classmates. I asked her, "You said you were a 'C' and 'D' student. Why was that? Is it that you weren't doing your work?"

Buddha replied, "It was like 'cause I like let things get to me in the classroom. Like if this person say something to me, I kept an attitude and be ready to fight them and things like that. But it wasn't nothing cause of the work. It's because I let other people get to me."

"Were you considered a behavior problem?" I asked, trying to ascertain whether her attitude was an outward manifestation.

"Well, yeah," Buddha admitted.

I wanted to know if she was the perpetrator, or if she was defending herself, "Did you start a lot of fights?"

"Uh-uh," she answered, meaning no. "It was like, 'cause I have like a quick attitude problem. Like anything could just make me snap."

Even today Buddha still has a short temper. I asked if she still found herself in conflicts. She explained, "Anything could just like if somebody be like, hey, I don't like her or something. And I try to ignore it for a minute, but if a person keep going on, then it make me snap and then I be ready to fight you."

"So basically, you throw the first punch as a result of something that was said, but they instigated the fight because they started the argument?" I asked to clarify how she was thinking about who was responsible for the scuffles.

"Right," she said.

She was a frequent visitor to the discipline office due to all of the fighting and bickering. "Sometimes when I like fight in the school there, they like, well, you finna [about to] get suspended or whatever. I be like, 'Oh, you all could suspend me or whatever, and I'll just leave out the building.' Like, if they going to suspend, what's my point of still staying here?"

So Buddha would leave the school building before she was dismissed by the disciplinarian. When Buddha was pregnant, her attitude in class grew worse, "When I was pregnant and I was in school, even my friends—my closest friends—I had attitudes with them, didn't want to be bothered with nobody. And if the teacher say something's wrong with me, I'd be snapping on the teachers and stuff. And I was just snapping on the teachers and stuff."

"Were you fighting then?" I questioned, wondering if the fact that she was pregnant discouraged her from fighting.

"It'd be a couple of fights that I had in school while I was pregnant....And then I had to fight them 'cause I didn't want them to be like spouting off, ain't going to do it because I'm pregnant and then let that person think they going to just get all over me without saying nothing, 'cause I thought, 'I ain't going to be a punk. I ain't going to be afraid of nobody.' [That's the] only thing I could do here. 'Cause if you afraid of somebody, that person going to run you your whole life. And I feel that I can't be afraid of nobody 'cause I don't want nobody to run my life. Like I say this, I can't take a problem for nobody else. That's why I try to keep away from niggas [slang for men] and females because I don't want—like if I'm out with a person, they did something wrong, and the person put it on me. I can't take the problem for another person. So I just had to go to school like, 'No, I don't want to be a punk when I was pregnant, I don't want to be punked by you. Don't come, don't talk to me, none of this.'"

"What kind of things put you in a bad mood?" I asked Buddha.

"I guess things, just the baby or whatever. I don't know, 'cause I just had like attitude for no reason. And I be looking at myself like, 'Why am I having an attitude like this?' Then when I did have attitudes, and the teachers is like sending me to the principal's office, and the principal ask, 'Well, why do you have a attitude?' I used to tell her, 'I don't know, I just have one.' [The principal would ask] 'You don't know what reason you have?' I was like, 'No.' I didn't know the reason why I be having an attitude. I just be catching an attitude, like quick. And I was like, 'Get away from me.' Somebody could be standing next to me, I'd be like, 'Get away from me, you stink.' I would just bust on someone with something like that, and they would be mad, really mad. Like, oh, well, you all shouldn't like do this. And then when I'd like calm down, I used to be like, 'Man, I'm sorry, I had an attitude then. I don't know what's the reason I had an attitude, but I'm sorry.' And they be like, 'Okay, that girl is crazy. Don't nobody know what be wrong with her. She just be getting an attitude, lashing out.'"

Buddha was frequently involved in fights, but she fought less when she was pregnant, "Before I was pregnant, it was like every other day I was in a fight. I was suspended about four or five times a year but I fought more than that. Every day, I mean, you know, teachers would like calm me down. Be like, yeah, okay, 'You need to stop fighting.' And sometimes teachers would be like, 'Okay, I don't care.'"

Buddha clearly describes a behavioral disorder; however, like Celina, she was never referred to special education services for evaluation.

Boredom with School

Buddha stated that she was often bored with school, not because of the type of work that they were doing, but because of the lack of work, "Sometimes I was bored with it [school]. Like when we didn't have nothing to do, and the teachers be sitting there doing nothing. And I'd be like, 'This is like boring.'"

Because I found it difficult to believe that teachers would sit at their desks without assigning work, I asked her if she was referring to substitute teachers, "Teachers would do this, or are you talking about substitutes?"

Buddha clarified, "When we have a substitute assignment. It was boring, like we didn't have nothing to do so we just sitting here."

Normally classrooms would not have substitutes on a regular basis; however, Buddha's comment caused me to think that she frequently had substitute teachers, "Did you have a lot of substitutes?"

"Yeah, 'cause like two of our teachers left so in those classes, we done had different teachers for about two months. We had just different teachers in them two classrooms. And that was like boring." Buddha's classes, like so many inner city schools, lacked permanent teachers and were staffed by uncertified teachers instead. Such a lack definitely impacts student learning and interest, though it remains a problem in urban school settings.

Attendance

Though Buddha attended school, she missed days frequently. I attempted to get an estimate of the days she missed, "How many days a month would you say you missed school?"

Her forehead wore a frown as she was thinking, "I'd say about three, four days. Probably not even that because you can't miss...10 days you can't miss, they'll [the school] drop you. So I would like once a month or something like that I'd like ditch or something. I didn't want to take it to the edge and then they'll drop you."

Cutting School

Buddha often cut school for no particular reason, "Yeah, I cut school a few times," she said.

"And why would you cut?" I asked.

"I don't know. Just 'cause, I don't know. Just to be doing something, me and my friends, we all did, like me and my sister and my cousins and my friends, we'd all just go, we just be in the park or, you know, we'll go just go places like that. And play on the stuff, like that."

Buddha attended school with her sister and cousins, and they often persuaded her to cut school. She described them as a distraction, "I was a problem child. I was a good student. Well, first I was a good student, you could catch me in the classroom doing all my work. And then when I like ditched, I let my cousins and my sisters and them make me ditch cause we all just went to the same school, that was the neighborhood school. We would all go there. And [they would] walk past the classroom like, 'Come on, you can go with us,' or something like that. And I let them interrupt me. And it was like I would be like I was trapped. And then I let them, like, influence me in doing other things and stuff like that."

Some of the things they influenced her to do was drink and smoke marijuana, "I always, you know, hang out in the area around my auntie's house with my auntie and my cousins about my same age. My auntie and them, they was about 28 or 29 or something like that. They did drink and stuff in the house, we would be smoking a blunt [marijuana wrapped in cigar paper] or something, but that's about it."

Unlike most high schools, many elementary schools do not change classes. Instead, one teacher teaches all subjects to the students. This was true for Buddha's school; therefore, she did not have the opportunity to cut classes, she cut school for the entire day.

Though Buddha lacked adult supervision, her grandmother would reprimand her when she cut school. The other children who cut cleverly intercepted phone calls that the attendance office made to their parents to notify them of absences; Buddha was not that fortunate.

"Did your grandmother ever know you were taking off from school?"

"Yeah, she knew 'cause it's like a phone thing," she said. "Like when you miss school, there is a recording. You pick up the phone, and they'll say, 'Your child have missed school today.' She found out like this. We be like, 'Well, it wasn't nothing to do at school so we just left. We didn't want to come home 'cause wasn't nobody there. We ain't got no keys,' stuff like that."

"What would she do about it?" I asked.

"She wasn't around to do nothing. She just be like, 'Well, yeah, I know you all can't be doing that 'cause you all be dumb for life.' We'd listen sometimes, sometimes we won't. I feel like Granny, I think she really did care 'cause the fussing she used to make when we used to ditch. She used to get real mean with it. Just look like real mean. She didn't never whip us or nothing, but she has a mean attitude," Buddha emphasized.

Teachers

Buddha's teachers were very strict, and from her description, seemed concerned with keeping order in the classroom, sometimes through assigning a lot of work. In fact, when I asked her to describe her teachers, the first thing that she mentioned was their disciplinary temperament, "They was like kind of strict. Some of them were strict. Some of them just let you do whatever you wanted to do. Some of them, you know, just give you work, tell you to do it, don't help you with it. And some of them, they help you with it."

Though the teachers were strict, Buddha maintained that they were fair with the students, "How would you say the teachers treated the students?"

"Fair," she answered. "You know, they wasn't that, let one student do something and then don't let the other student do it. They were like—they will treat everybody—they'll do everybody equal. It won't be no differences, they'll treat everybody equal."

"So they didn't have any favorites like the person, you know, teacher's pet or something like that?"

Buddha confirmed, "Right, they had no favorites."

As a result, she never had any personal problems with the teachers, where she felt as though she was singled out, though she was constantly in trouble because of the frequent fighting.

Buddha's assertion that they treated everyone fair was not entirely true, because she later told me that the teachers seemed to administer harsher treatment for boys when they misbehaved. There were differences in the way in which girls and boys were treated. I asked, "Like, do you think boys and girls are treated the same?"

Buddha admitted there was a difference, "Well, when I was there, girls kind of like got away with like a little bit of everything, and boys didn't. Boys, every time the boys did something wrong, they would get in trouble for it. Because we had like teachers like Mr. Hughes, they wouldn't accept the boys doing no wrong. Because the boys, they'd like, they'll try to sneak and smoke weed in the bathroom and stuff, so they had to be more stricter on the boys than the girls. So I think the girls like had it kind of gooder than the boys did." Though there was unequal treatment, she thought that the boys deserved it because they smoked marijuana on the school grounds, while she and her friends smoked it off of the school grounds.

"Who do you think participated more in school, boys or girls?" I asked, because I was curious whether the teachers gave more one-on-one attention to the boys.

"Girls," she replied. "Because most boys really don't like to go to school. Most boys like to spend time outside and trying drugs and go ditch school, go smoke weed. I don't know. That's my experience 'cause a lot of my cousins, you know, do it. So that's mostly, I think, girls like going to school more than the boys do. Like that little saying they say, what's that? Boys are from Jupiter—what's that?"

I completed the cliché, "Women are from Venus, men are from Mars."

"Right, that little saying like that, I believe that it's true. Because boys, they like really don't have it all. They don't click really well and the females, they kind of do...You know, 'cause females, I think they'll understand more than a man will."

Though Buddha was a self-described "problem child," some of the closest relationships she had were with her teachers. They were the adults that she went to when she had a problem, because her parents were absent and her grandmother did not have time. Hence, her teachers were like surrogate parents. When I asked her to describe her relationship with her teachers she told me, "[I felt close to] some of them, there were only four, 'cause they were knowing me for a long time, and they knew how I was. And if I had a problem, I feel I can go tell them. You know, whatever I was feeling that day, they could tell me like, 'Okay, well, this is what you need to do such and such, etc.' A couple of times I went to them with problems I think."

"What kind of problems were they?" I asked.

"Like whatever I was feeling that day. Whatever happened that day, I could go tell them, and they'd tell me, 'Well, this is what you should do. Just like the negatives, just stay away from them. This is what you should do.' You know, [they would] explain it to me."

The conversations she described seemed to be the kind one would expect to occur between a child and his or her parents. It seemed as though her relationship with the teachers seemed more like a parental one, so I asked if they were fulfilling a void for her, "Did you have anybody else in your life at that time, like when you had a problem, someone that you could go and talk to that you felt could help you?"

"Uh-uh," she replied. So, Buddha was in a situation in which she lacked adult guidance, though she was able to find some consolation with her teachers. Due to her lack of a guiding relationship, she kept her pregnancy a secret from everyone. She also hid the fact that she was sexually active. As a result, she was nine months pregnant before anyone knew.

Pregnancy and Dropping Out

Buddha was pregnant with her son at the age of 14. As stated earlier, she did not have close relationships with adults in her family, and though she was close to some of her teachers, she did not share her pregnancy with them. She kept the secret from her cousins and friends, "When you got pregnant, who did you tell? Did you tell anybody?"

Buddha shook her head and said, "Didn't tell nobody...not a soul."

I was surprised that someone so young could deal with the physical and emotional stress of pregnancy without sharing it with anyone. "Really? Was that hard?"

"Not really. 'Cause anybody, they used to look at me, like, 'Are you pregnant?' I used to tell them, 'No.' I used to tell them, 'It's cause I got asthma. I got asthma, and I had some like the little pills called prednisone, and they can blow you up [meaning gain weight].' I would tell them, 'No, just my medication do that.'"

Buddha was in her ninth month before anyone knew she was pregnant. Prior to that, she was able to camouflage her stomach with baggy clothes. "What happened was my grandmother...took me to the doctor. I said I didn't want her to find out. 'Cause she was like, 'Come on, we finna go to the doctor'... So I had one of my other cousins take the test and it came out negative. So she was like, 'Okay, she not pregnant.' So I say about five months later, this was when I was nine months, we went back to the doctor 'cause everybody kept saying, 'That girl is pregnant,' so she did it so fast, I couldn't do nothing. I was like, 'Well, I'm nine months anyway, might as well go ahead and let her know.' So we go to the doctor. She found out I'm pregnant, but the doctor told her I was still five months pregnant, which I wasn't. So that same day that she found out, I went in labor. It shocked her, that's how she found out I was pregnant. And it was such a shock to her because I was the first one out of all my cousins, you know, to get pregnant, and it was like a shock to her. She really wasn't saying anything about it. After the baby was here, she's like, 'Well, it's said and done with so I really can't say nothing.'"

Though her grandmother accepted the child, she felt that Buddha should shoulder the responsibility of motherhood. As a result, she made her stay at home to care for her son; therefore, it was impossible for her to return to school.

"I left school in my ninth month. After I had my baby, I didn't go back to school. Only reason I didn't finish school was because I like had to stay home with my baby, take care of my baby 'cause there wasn't nobody else going to do it. So that's the only reason I didn't finish school, because I had a baby young. Everybody in my house had to go to school. Everybody in my house had to go to work so I had to take care of that responsibility. That's the only reason why I didn't finish school. I thought about it like, 'I should just stay in school.' I used to ask my grandma can she like pay for a baby-sitter or something. She was saying, 'No, you got to stay here and take care of your own responsibility 'cause you don't want nobody else taking care of your baby.' So I took heed to that, you know, and I stayed at home. And then I used to think like every day like, 'Man, I need to go to school.'"

Due to the lack of support with her son and her grandmother's refusal to hire a babysitter, Buddha never returned to school and never received an eighth grade diploma.

Survival Sex: "I Needed Some Place To Stay"

Buddha learned about prostitution when she was 10 years old. Some of the women in her family and in her neighborhood were prostitutes. I asked her, "How did you first learn about prostitution?"

Buddha replied, "[By] looking at the females in my own family, just looking at them. It's like how bad they used to be walking around naked and stuff like that...I was like, 'I never want to be like that.'"

"How old were you?" I asked.

"I'd say about I first ever seen a prostitute and my grandma explained to me what it was, I think I was about 10 years old. I realized she looked bad and she really don't need to be out here like that."

The first prostitutes that she knew personally were her aunt's friends that she met when she was 12, "One of my aunties, she used to have friends that was prostitutes. They weren't like on the street corner prostitutes, but they was like well-kept prostitutes."

The term "well-kept" can refer to one's status through material wealth. Oftentimes it is used as a descriptor for women whose male companions provide the material items. However, I asked Buddha to define how she was using the term, "Well-kept by whom?"

Buddha explained that she was using the term differently, "By theyselves. You know, kept theyselves well. You know, they ain't out there looking like a hot mess and all that."

"Did they have pimps?" I questioned.

"I'm not sure if they did, but most of the females around us didn't have pimps. They just used to work for theyselves," she said. So, prostitution took on a different form in her community, as women brokered themselves and kept the money.

"These women that you're talking about, did they stand out on the corners?" I asked.

"Which ones, the well-kept or the hot mess?" She asked, describing call girls and street prostitutes

"The well-kept ones," I clarified.

"Oh, no," she answered emphatically. "The well-kept ones, they didn't use to be on the corners. They used to be downtown or something like that."

I asked Buddha to tell me about her impressions of prostitution at that time and she stated, "I used to put it in different ways. I used to call the well-kept prostitutes, I used to call them call girls. And the [street] prostitutes, I used to, them hot mess ones, I just used to call them straight prostitutes. 'Cause to me it was like a difference...'cause the prostitutes, the hot mess ones, they used to be on the corner doing any and everything. You'd see them real dirty and everything, smoking on the corners, in the hallways. Ain't got no where to go. The well-kept ones, or I used to just call them call girls 'cause they don't be out there like that. They ain't on drugs or whatever. They just, you know, be intimate with all type of people. That's how I used to tell 'cause they kept theyself clean, wasn't on drugs or nothing like that, had they own apartments and stuff."

Because she was making such a clear distinction between the two types of prostitutes, and it seemed as though she respected the call girls more, I delved deeper into the value judgments she seemed to be making, "So what did you think about them, the call girls?"

"Really, I didn't think too much of them, 'cause I really don't even be thinking about prostitutes back then. My mind don't even be on that. Yeah, I wouldn't say I had respect, and I wouldn't say I didn't have respect. You know, it was like a so-so thing," she answered.

However, it was clear to me that she thought that the call girls were more tolerable than the street prostitutes because they were not "out in the open" as she had referred to it in one of our earlier conversations. This distinction of being "in the open" is important as it is connected to her ideas, judgments, and definitions of prostitution, as she later fails to self-describe her trading sex with a man for shelter as prostitution. However, when I described survival sex as trading sex for shelter, clothes, food, or other items needed to survive, she agreed that she was indeed involved in survival sex.

"This is the Only Person I Can Go To:" Survival Sex

When I first met Buddha, I told her I was conducting a study on female dropouts and prostitution, and she listened patiently as I explained the study. I went on to describe prostitution in the way it was described at a conference I attended where survival sex was explained to me. The young women involved in survival sex who were present at the conference explained that many young women exchange sex for food, shelter, clothing, safety, and so forth. Hence, survival sex is a more acceptable descriptor to these young women. They tend to differentiate themselves from prostitutes, with the difference hinging upon the fact that they usually do not receive cash for the sex. Also, they usually do not have a pimp.

Buddha agreed with this definition of prostitution and admitted that she had been involved in survival sex at one time. I asked her to describe her situation at the time she was involved in survival sex.

Buddha began to explain, "That was like 'cause me and my grandma, we was like in bad times—this was when my baby was about six months old. I was 15. Me and her had got into a argument over something, and I told her something and she like told me, 'Well, if you don't like it, 'cause that's like how it's gone be then, you should leave if you feel like that.' I told her, 'If you feel like that, then maybe I shouldn't be here.' So me and my baby left. There's this nigga I used to be messing with a long, long time ago, and he always liked me 'cause he used to always give me money and stuff. So I [and her son] went over to his house."

"Was he your boyfriend?" I asked to understand the context of their relationship.

"He wasn't no boyfriend. He just the type of person that liked me. Had a real big, old crush on me ever since I was a little girl. He liked me. So I was like, okay, well, I'm going to go over to his house. He let me stay over there and everything. I stayed, you know, with him for about two weeks. Yeah, two weeks. So it all boiled down to the point that, [he said] 'Okay, you staying here, you need to give me some [sex].' And, okay, when he said, 'I'm like okay, it's cool because I have been staying here with you,' and I gave him that [sex]. And I was angry with myself that I was doing it. I'm like this did not feel right to me. So I went back home. I didn't like it at all," she said looking disgusted.

"Have you ever been in a situation like that again or something similar to that?" I asked to understand if she often found herself in survival sex situations.

"Uh-uh," she answered. "'Cause I don't even let myself to go out like this. I was feeling like, 'Why did I just do that?' And I'm like there was no reaction [to the sex]. That's how it seemed to me 'cause, you know, you don't think about it when you do it, but afterwards, you just start to thinking," she said meaning the full magnitude of what she was doing was occurring to her.

At the time, Buddha didn't feel as though she had any other place to go, and she did not have the financial means to take care of herself, "When you went over to his house to stay with him, did you feel like you had any place else to go?"

"No, not really," she answered shaking her head. "'Cause I didn't want to go to my auntie and them houses. So I was like, okay, this is the only person I can go to."

"Did you have any way of supporting yourself at that time financially?"

"No, uh-uh," she answered explaining that her financial situation is the same today, "Now, I still don't have any way, like not financially 'cause I don't get public aid or nothing like this. So my grandma watch the kids, we supposed to go early this morning [to the public aid office]. But everybody like overslept. Me, my cousin, and my grandma, all three of us were going; so she said tomorrow morning we going to try to go."

Education Needed for Survival

Buddha has never received public assistance for herself and her son, though she was planning to apply at the time I met her. However, she attempted to secure employment on many occasions and was unsuccessful. She found that her lack of education was a barrier. Her fruitless job-search experiences have led her to understand the value of education. She has always thought that education was important, both before and after she dropped out; however, she now knows that it is imperative for economic survival in this society. She described why she values education, "Because, say if you get a job and you have to...read. Even numbers or anything, you still have to read. You got to know how to fill out a job application and all that so education is very important. No matter who teaches it to you, you still need to learn it. So if you're going to go out there in the streets, you got to learn something. You not just streetwise, but you got to have, you know, math-wise and all that, too. You just can't be streetwise 'cause streetwise ain't good enough. So you need your education no matter what you do. You still need it."

She described one of her attempts to find employment, "I wasn't able to get a job. I filled out an application and all that, but I don't think they never called back. They never called me or whatever. So I just never worried about it. Like, okay, 'cause when I put on the application, I put eighth grade is the only grade I completed. And I think that's like hard, you know, you got to have a high school diploma going to school. You have to have some type of diploma, and I don't have one of those. So that's kind of hard."

Once, Buddha was able to find a job working in a clothing store, unfortunately she had to leave because her manager was sexually harassing her, "I didn't like it too much because the manager supposed to be helping me, but he used to always like try to hit on me. So I didn't like it."

The Community

Prostitution in the Community

Prostitution was commonplace in the community in which Buddha grew up. In fact, there were quite a few prostitutes in the apartment complex she lived in. "We had about, I'd say you had about 15 prostitutes around there." Her complex was known for drug dealing and prostitution, and sometimes the two worked in conjunction, as the drugs drew the prostitutes and the women needed to continue to work to afford the drugs.

Buddha described the cycle, "They had prostitutes running in and out, drug dealers running in and out, drug users running in and out there...The prostitutes just used to go in there and buy stuff from them."

Buddha described high rates of unemployment in her community, "Nobody around there have a job...nobody," she emphasized.

As a result of the high unemployment rate, many women used prostitution as a way of supporting themselves and their children, "So how were they taking care of themselves and the kids?"

She replied, "Well, prostituting. That's how they did it."

As she stated earlier, some of the women in her family were involved in prostitution; however, she had friends and peers who were involved as well, "This girl, Alice, we grew up with, she used to go to school with us. She was a straight 'A' student. She dropped out of school. She got three kids now. She use drugs and she a prostitute."

I thought Buddha recently mentioned her in another conversation; however, I found out that this was another girl she knew. "I think you were telling me about that the other day. You said you knew her, but you all weren't real close. Is that the one you were talking about? Remember, I asked you did you have any friends or did you know anybody that involved in prostitution?"

"That was another girl," she answered. It was becoming clear that young girls prostituting was commonplace in her neighborhood. The other girl to whom she was referring was a 13-year-old girl with whom she attended school who had become a street prostitute. Buddha was adamant about the fact that many of the prostitutes that she knew were young women, "...the girls around there are all either real young, like 12. Ain't none of them over the age of 21. They doing drugs and prostitution. Like if you can be out there at about five in the morning, you can go to the gas station and you can walk out there and you could see—nothing but young girls out there. They prostitutes. And you wouldn't even know that they're young 'cause they look older. But they be young as ever. Talking about they can be real young, and you be like, 'Oh, she old,' but she don't be older. She be young, about 16, 17 years old. Don't none of them be over the age of 21."

"How do you think they get turned out into prostitution?"

"I don't know how they get turned out there. I can just put it on their family. That's the only way I can see."

Buddha described the dynamics among prostitutes in her area, "Young girls and older women, they was prostituting together. They acted like they was real close friends. The youngest one was 12 years old on the block and she died, oh, about a couple of weeks after her birthday, after she just turned 13. Somebody killed her. They found her in the alley."

By this point, Buddha mentioned that a couple of the prostitutes whom she had known had been killed, it turned out that the neighborhood in which she lived was the area in Chicago where there was a serial killer preying on prostitutes during the summer of 2000. She described how the serial killings impacted the community, "I know plenty of prostitutes or call girls who have been killed over the past two years. So I don't think it's good idea to be out there prostituting...one lady they found—'cause I remember—everybody in my family, we remember this girl. She was about 18 years old. She used to be a prostitute, smoke and all that because before we moved, she used to be in our building in the hallway and stuff freaking out, whatever they want to call it. And this summer, we found out that she had died. Somebody had her naked...they had her strangled over the train tracks right on the other side of the railing. She was just hanging there. This other girl named Maya, she used to be a prostitute around there. Somebody found her in the alley with her throat slit, she was about I'd say about 27. The other one [on the train tracks], she was about 19, 20. It was in the news, but I don't know if it was *on* [italics added] the news, but it was in the newspapers."

"Did the police do anything about it to let the folks know what was going on?" I asked because I was familiar with the case; in fact, the Federal Bureau of Investigation was working on the case.

"Oh, everybody around, they knew what was going on 'cause they had put like little flags up in the stores and stuff. They knew what was going on. At the time, it was about 10 murders. There was a lot of prostitutes being killed. I knew about maybe three or four of them, but that's it."

Work and the Community

Buddha's community had many small stores and shops; however, they did not employ many residents from the community. She stated, "[The community had] grocery stores, pawn shops, hardware stores, gas stations, and restaurants. We had pool halls and stuff. A lot of stores were there." Therefore, the residents did not have many opportunities for employment within their neighborhood.

The two service agencies present in the area were a drug rehabilitation center and the Women, Infants, and Children office (WIC), which provides milk and food for impoverished women and their children. Though these services were provided free of charge, Buddha maintained that people rarely used the services, "It was like, some of the people was like ashamed go to the WIC office, so mostly nobody went there. Everybody look around. They never go to the WIC office." However, she used the WIC services for her son.

Buddha stated that most of the people in the community did not work. As a result, the crime rate in the area was high; many people were involved in the drug trade and many women were involved in prostitution.

The Community's Idea of Success

The standard of success within the community was connected to one's success in their delinquent activities, according to Buddha. I asked her, "What things does a person have to own or accomplish in order to be considered successful in the community you grew up in?"

She quickly answered, "Got to be a drug dealer, a thug, or you got to be the hardest person on the block."

"Hard meaning what?" I asked, needing further clarification.

"Like over everybody. Got everybody scared of you or whatever, like that."

"What kind of things do you have to have?" I prompted.

"Money, cars...Any new car that just came out...Cadillac trucks, all that around there, everybody just had to have one of them rides," she explained.

"If you wanted to become successful, what would you have to do?" I asked, meaning anyone one in the community.

"Start off from an eight-ball nigga [a drug runner] and work your way up [through the drug industry]...you don't have to be gang related."

The Family

Buddha lived in the house with her extended family, including her sisters, aunts, uncles, cousins, and grandmother. Though it was a four bedroom apartment, 15 people lived there. There was constant traffic through the house, though most of the adults worked and the children attended school. Buddha's grandmother raised her, as neither of her parents was active in her life.

Her Father

Though Buddha lived with her paternal grandmother, she did not have much contact with her father. However, her father lived with them for a short while. During the time he was there, Buddha described their relationship as strained due to his efforts to control her and her sisters. Her description of her father was less than favorable, as he was a recidivist offender. "Tell me about your father, " I asked.

Buddha began, "My father had 13 children....He was like one of those fathers...who had problems. He had been to jail for...attempted murder, drugs. He just got out of jail like a year ago. He was in jail for about, I'd say two-and-a-half years. He shot somebody....The longest time I think he stayed was something like eight years, I think that was attempted murder [charge] he had."

"What was your relationship with your father like?" I asked, though she told me that they did not have much of a relationship since he spent much of her life in jail.

She shook her head saying, "I never did like my father....Maybe 'cause he was one of those fathers that when he got out of jail, he used to try to be strict with me and sister. And then my daddy, while he be younger and he was like at home and not in jail, he used to tell me to get mad at the family like the family would get mad at him. They'd tell him to get out the house or whatever 'cause he like to argue when he drunk. And he'd get mad and he'd tell me and my sister, he ain't got no daughters. All he got is sons. And me and my sister used to be like, 'Okay'. So me and my sister, we wouldn't even talk to him. Till this day, we still don't talk to him. We have no conversation. He'll come over our house, we'll go into another room 'cause we don't want to talk to him.... He really don't like his girls. He like his boys, that's what he say. So that's how much I can tell you about him, 'cause I really don't know much about him."

Buddha does not have a relationship with her father, and he now lives with his wife and some of his other children.

Her Mother

Buddha has never lived in the same house with her mother; today her mother lives with her husband and two other children. Her relationship with her mother is as strained as the relationship with her father, due to her mother's abandonment of her and her sisters. Buddha explained, "My mother, she gave us to my grandmother when we were born and we were about a year old, me and my sister....My mother, she kept one, the youngest baby. She gave me and my other sister to my granny. My daddy, he was in jail at the time she gave us to my granny. So after that, we never seen her till about three years ago. We just started talking back with her....I seen my mama like two weeks ago, last week. She work at a pet store."

"Would you say you have a relationship with her?" I asked.

"I really don't even talk to her like that...I see her like four times out of the month. She just calls and see how me and my sister doing and her grandkids are doing. I really don't say nothing to her....Ain't too much I could tell you about her."

Buddha's mother was 14 years old when she had her sister and 15 when she gave birth to Buddha. Buddha does not consider her mother's youth as a valid excuse for abandoning her and her sister. I thought that she would have been able to empathize with her mother since she had her son at the same age; however, it is her love for her son that made it impossible for her to understand how her mother could have left her children. As Buddha states, he is her only reason for living.

Her Son

Buddha gave birth to her son when she was 14 years old. She had to leave school to take care of him and has not returned. Though she regrets that she has not been able to complete school, she does not regret having her son and loves him dearly.

She beamed, "I love my son, and my son love me. And he tell me that every day. I got a real good relationship with my baby. I think that I'm a good mother 'cause I take care of my baby....Like 'cause I feel that's the only thing I'm living for is my baby. That boy, that's the only person I'm living for is my child. And can't nobody take that away."

The Psychological

Buddha has overcome a great deal of trauma in her life; however, she is resilient. She shared with me that she was gang-raped by her ex-boyfriend and three of his friends. When I asked how she deals with the trauma of it, she replied, "I don't think of it." Though she told me that she often, "pushes stuff out" of her mind, her primary methods of dealing with her issues are writing poetry and listening to music. She has never been to counseling, though some of her emotions continue to surface. For example, she still has difficulty coping with her parents' abandonment, particularly her mother's.

"The worst thing...was just my parents not being around. That's the only thing that really affected me growing up. And I'm still like having problems with it," she told me during out first interview. However, in our last interview, she stated that she was no longer disturbed by her mother's desertion.

"It's cool with me. When I was young, as I was growing up, it used to upset me. But now that I'm older, it don't even bother me....Like I used to ask my grandmama and them all the time like, 'Why did she leave me and my sister like that?' I used to just ask them, and I still got a lot of questions like that." From this comment, it is clear that she still has some issues with her mother; however, she has not discussed them with her. She carries them around with her, trying to "push it out" of her mind.

Hope for Tomorrow

When I met Buddha, she had enrolled in a G.E.D. course the previous day. Due to her inability to obtain gainful employment, her desire to pursue her education has increased. Though she realizes that it takes many years of schooling, she wants to become a lawyer. "It's something that I had ever since I was younger. I always wanted to be a lawyer, always. I think they can really help a person out that really didn't do nothing. And I be looking at it like, okay. My uncle used to say, 'You want to be a lawyer so bad, you need to watch these TV shows. They'd probably really help you.' You know, sometime he make jokes, whatever and stuff. And that started it out because some lawyers, they really can help a person if they like in a murder that they can't get off and don't nobody know what happened."

I explained to Buddha that television is not a sound depiction of the practice of law, and that lawyers spend most of their time outside of the courtroom. That did not sway her; she still had hopes of becoming a lawyer. I believe with the right guidance and support, it is possible that her dream can become a reality. I reflect on the words in the final verse of her favorite song, "Get It Together," "Thought it will never change but this time moved on/An ugly duckling grew up to be a swan/And now it just burns in your backaches/Because now beads are showing upon your face/But you're never really happy/And you'll never be whole/Until you see the beauty in growing hope," and I am amazed at Buddha's resilience and undying hope.

Understanding Buddha: An Interpretation

Undiagnosed Behavioral Disorder

Buddha was often involved in fights and verbal conflict at school. As she stated, she was suspended four times for fighting and was frequently sent to the discipline and/or principal's office regarding her behavior. She described not being able to control her anger and rage at times and that her temper grew worse when she was pregnant. She was a self-described behavior problem; however, she was never referred for a special education evaluation. Instead, she was allowed to disrupt the classroom. The teachers' failure to refer her for an evaluation for a behavioral disorder harkens to the issues researchers raise about girls' referral rates for special education services lagging behind that of boys (Wehmeyer & Schwartz, 2001; Anderson, 1997; Andrews, Wisniewski, & Mulick, 1997; Reschly, 1996; Russo & Talbert-Johnson, 1997; Harmon, Stockton, & Contrucci, 1992).

It is interesting that Buddha was not referred because other research suggests that the reason that girls are not referred is because they are usually not disruptive to the classroom environment (Wehmeyer & Schwartz, 2001). However, Buddha was highly disruptive.

Education as a Barrier

Buddha dropped out of school prior to receiving her eighth grade diploma; therefore, she does not have any educational credentials. This lack of education, coupled with her inexperience, left her without any means of economic sustenance. Also, though she qualifies for aid to families with dependent children, she has not applied for any benefits. As a result, she is totally reliant upon her grandmother and other people to financially care for her and her son.

Buddha realizes that she needs some source of income to survive, so she has applied for jobs; however, she is unable to secure a job due to what she perceives as a lack of both education and experience. In an economy that is becoming more skills-based and technologically advanced, people like Buddha are quickly becoming displaced. Though she realizes her lack of education is a barrier, she had not received a G.E.D. at the time I met her. As a result of a lack of income, she found herself involved in survival sex when she was asked to leave her grandmother's house.

One of the primary reasons that prostitutes cite for entering and remaining in prostitution is the lack of education and/or job skills, and the same is true for Buddha.

Cycle of Teen Pregnancy and Lack of Family Support

Buddha's family has a history of teenage pregnancy, as her grandmother had her father during her teenage years, her mother gave birth to her when she was 14, and Buddha had her son when she was 14 as well. Her sister also gave birth to her son before she was 18 years old. Though I am not sure as to why her grandmother and mother did not complete school, Buddha did not return to school because she did not have anyone to care for her son. In fact, her grandmother discouraged her from having someone else care for her son. Therefore, teenage pregnancy has had an effect on the women in her family's abilities to complete and/or continue their education. Though public aid provides day care funds for young women with children who are working or in school, Buddha did not take advantage of these services because she was not a public aid recipient. However, Buddha was aware of the services that public aid provides.

Part Three

Getting an Understanding

CHAPTER EIGHT

Getting an Understanding

The Disconnection between the School
and the Community

Many political and educational plans have failed because their authors designed them according to their own personal views of reality, never once taking into account (except as mere objects of their actions) the men-in-a-situation to whom their program was ostensibly directed. (Freire, 1998, p.75)

Carmella, Celina, and Buddha were raised in socioeconomically disadvantaged communities that suffered from high rates of unemployment and crime coupled with low levels of education. The women told me due to the economic situations in which many of the residents found themselves, destitute and relying on government subsidies for their survival with minimal education and job skills, many people became and remained involved in criminal activities such as drug dealing and prostitution. In fact, many of their family members were involved in these activities: Carmella's family was infamous for its dealings in the drug trade, her father was a pimp, and Buddha's aunt was a prostitute. Though none of Celina's immediate family members were involved in criminal activities, many of the people in her community were, and she admitted to selling drugs with her godsister at the time she met her pimp.

From all accounts of their community environments, many residents' lives were the antithesis of what schools considered to be successful and well-adjusted citizens; Carmella's teachers often told their students that they needed to get an education so that they could move out of their community. These teachers stressed that they needed to break cycles of poverty and crime through educational attainment, and leave their community to live a better life. While it should certainly be the hope of teachers that students build a life free of poverty and crime and rise above their socioeconomic barriers, positioning that hope against the realities of their students' everyday lives and negating the culture of their home and community environment alienates students and is ineffective as a tool for increasing students' value of education. In the case of these three women, all of whom are African American, this devaluation of their home and community culture also means the negation of their cultural identity as African Americans, for while it is true that African Americans share a common culture, each community has its own specific culture.

As I have written elsewhere (Clardy et al., 2001), the duality of the lives of African American students is present in the ringing of every school bell. Each school day represents the shedding of one face and the application of another, as students leave parts of their cultural selves on the playground to embark on the endless journey of assimilation, a journey which includes learning the "proper way of speaking and being" (based on Eurocentric models) in American society. They soon learn that the manner in which they speak at home is not acceptable because it is not "standard" or "proper" English. They learn that the cultural practices that are present in their lives are not the norm; therefore, they become disconnected from their learning experience (Woodson, 1933; Delpit, 1995; Ladson-Billings, 1994, 1998; Foster, 1995). This often leads to a fragmented self, as students are faced with the paradox of their school identity not being appropriate at home and in social situations; likewise, their cultural selves are not acceptable at school (Fine, 1986; Fordham, 1988; Fordham & Ogbu, 1986). Thus, they live in the cracks between who they are and who society says that they are supposed to be. African American students soon learn that in order to survive in both of these worlds, they have to learn to "code switch," meaning to "move with facility between African American language and a standard form of English....role switching between school and home" (Ladson-Billings, 1998, p. 219).

Some African American educators posit that what it means to be "educated" for blacks is the renouncement of their culture (Asante, 1987; Ogbu, 1978, 1995). Evans states, "another price paid by the recipient of an education, and this is the personal cost of the process of deculturalisation, or de-Africanisation, whereby all personal expressions of one's original African culture are eliminated and [Euro-American] codes established instead....The price of a good education, a [Euro-American] education, in short, was and still is, the denial of one's Black cultural identity" (Evans, 1988, p. 185).

For students like Carmella, Celina, and Buddha, in school they face the negation of their African American culture and the specific culture of their community, which hold values that conflict with those of the school. In May's study on the influence of students' neighborhood values on their educational experience, he found that at the intersection of school, home, and community (including peers) exists conflict (1980). He concluded that when these conflicts are present, the most powerful influences are the home and community, stating that the possibility for conflict is at its greatest for students from socioeconomically disadvantaged backgrounds whose family and community members may have had limited success in their educational and work experience. This leads them to undervalue education and what he terms "pessimistic anticipatory socialization." Additionally, students from middle-class families who live in these predominantly working-class and poor communities reflect the same attitudes towards school.

Though May only considered socioeconomic status in his study, race and ethnicity are of great significance. In the case of African Americans, who suffer from racism and discrimination, many have attained high levels of education only to be unemployed and underemployed due to discrimination. When such incidents occur, space is created for pessimistic anticipatory socialization and education may become undervalued, not because it is deemed unimportant, but because it has not proven to be beneficial in an economic way. As one Native American student stated, "...As I got older, I realized that education for Indians meant nothing. There were no jobs, no opportunities. So why even try?" (Bowker, 1993, p.109). Many African American students living in socioeconomically disadvantaged communities echo the same sentiment.

Education is a long-term investment. In order for students to invest, there must be some future promise of remarkable benefit. If students who are from socioeconomically disadvantaged communities (as were Carmella, Celina, and Buddha) do not have visible representations and proof of those who have benefited from education, they are required to have faith that it will prove to be a wise investment for them. This faith is more difficult to muster when community members who have acquired economic success through criminal activity are more abundant than those who became successful through traditional means. The presence of people who achieved success through educational attainment is threatened when teachers and school personnel tell students that they should become educated so that they can leave their impoverished communities, thus creating a cycle of stripping communities of valuable resources.

In order for schools and communities to meet on a common ground, schools must seek to understand the cultures of the communities in which they are located. They must understand and attempt to address some of these issues, not negate them. While Celina and Buddha attended schools that they stated did not interact with the surrounding communities and impressed upon them their need to get an education so they could leave their communities, Carmella attended a school that was attuned to some of the needs of the students and community, as they had an in-school day care program for their students who were teen mothers (as many were).

Teachers as "Othermothers"

Patricia Hill Collins examines the dynamics of mothering relationships among women of color and children to whom they did not give birth (1990). Collins posits that this phenomenon of "othermothers" stems out of an African tradition that survived the detriment of slavery. The practice is a product of a culture in which the larger community is responsible for the welfare of its children, through community-based child care. It is a tradition in which women, whether they share biological ties (such as aunts, cousins, or other relatives) or not, take on the role of assisting in the welfare and development of the child. She explains that these relationships are formed regardless of the absence or presence of a biological mother. Though Collins centers her discussion of othermothering on the residential community, it is also present in relationships outside of the residential community. It is present in the relationship that many teachers have with their students, as was evidenced in the relationships both Carmella and Celina had with African American female teachers.

Carmella and Celina stated that they had close relationships with at least one of their teachers. Carmella's relationship with her dance teacher, Ms. Simpson, was of great importance to her. Ms. Simpson had a history with Carmella's family, as she had taught her mother and aunts as well. She described talking to her about personal problems. The relationship that Carmella shared with Ms. Simpson was not unusual; many students confided in her and looked to her for guidance. As Carmella stated, "Everybody liked Ms. Simpson. Her classroom just stayed crowded up for advice."

Celina described her relationship with her eighth-grade teacher as a mothering one. Ms. Hurston was always available to assist her female students with personal issues. She invited them to her home on the weekend for sleepovers and created a community among the girls and herself. She counseled the girls on issues that they faced, and encouraged them to talk to her about things that maybe they could not share with their parents. She did this not in an effort to replace those relationships, but to make sure that they were always able to receive the counsel of an adult. Celina described her as, "a shoulder to lean on." She could talk to her about personal problems because she felt safe with her. Even today, she has a relationship with Ms. Hurston. While in her class, Celina thrived. Though she was not sure, she stated that if she had had a relationship with a teacher like Ms. Hurston in high school, it's possible that she would not have dropped out.

While Ms. Hurston and Ms. Simpson shared the same racial background as Carmella and Celina, othermothering can take place across racial and ethnic backgrounds; I enjoyed this type of relationship with a White teacher throughout my high school experience.

Social Aggression Among Schoolgirls

In recent years, researchers have developed an interest in aggression and violence among girls (Wiseman, 2003; Eisner, 2002; Flanigan, 2002; Simmons, 2002; Vail, 2002; Artz, 1997). Many girls have begun to speak out about emotional and physical abuse inflicted upon them by their female peers due to their inability to integrate into social settings, or their desire to separate from certain factions of girls at school (Wiseman, 2003; Simmons, 2002; Vail, 2002). In some cases, physical violence is viewed as a rite of passage among girls, as can be seen in the case of senior girls in Northbrook, Illinois caught on videotape beating their junior peers (Dizon, 2003). As a result of these types of experiences, the academic value of schooling suffers; the violence that girls experience overshadows the actual learning process. Research on violence among girls suggests that once they become victims of repeated taunting, they tend to lose interest in the school and classroom experience and become socially withdrawn (Wiseman, 2003; Simmons, 2002). In many cases, they either transfer or leave the school system totally. In an extreme case, one victim of such abuse ended her own life (Toronto Star, 2001). As should be evident, the devastating effect that emotional and physical violence has on girls is of grave importance.

Carmella was a victim of this type of aggression. She had been in physical confrontations with girls at school for as long as she could remember. In elementary school, girls pulled her long, wavy braids because they were jealous of both the length and texture of her hair. When they could not pull it and inflict pain that way, they instigated fights. They hated her because of her hair, as hair historically has been coveted in African American culture (Ansariyah-Grace, 1995; Grayson, 1995; Boyd, 1994; Wilson, 1994). Carmella's experience with bullying and taunting is representative of what Banks (1997) discovered in his work on bullying at the elementary level; it is directed at anyone who is different. While Carmella's classmates were African American and lived in the same community, her long, wavy, textured hair made her different. This resentment followed her through high school and intensified as boys began to become attracted to her; creating another source of conflict. As an elementary school student, Carmella was terrified by this constant conflict. By the time she transitioned into high school, she was less terrified and less intimidated by the girls' threats and taunting. She fought whenever she was approached, because she was tired of being the victim. The issues with her female peers, coupled with her molestation and home life, led to her disgruntled attitude toward school and her personal life.

It never seemed to occur to Carmella that she was not responsible for dealing with the conflict with these girls on her own. Though these conflicts began in the classroom or some other area of the school, they were settled off school grounds through fights. She never spoke of telling the teachers or administrators about the fights. Since these fights started in class at times, some teachers had to have known about them or heard about the fights. However, Carmella never spoke of them intervening; no conferences, no suspensions, no truces.

The lack of adult intervention stems from the failure of teachers to address these behaviors of which many are aware, but do not want to get involved (Hansen & Smith, 2001; Banks, 1997). While many students feel that the teachers witness or know about the bullying, the students do not seek their help (as was true in Carmella's case). As a result of students' failure to report these incidents to teachers and/or administrators, the teachers mistakenly assume that the bullying is not detrimental to the student's life (Shakeshaft et al., 1998). She felt as though she had to deal with it on her own, since the actual fights usually took place off of school grounds. However, the school is responsible for the students' safety, especially if the impetus for the fight was a dispute that occurred at school.

Buddha's conflicts with her peers typically escalated into physical brawls; she stated that she was involved in a fight at least once a week. Buddha described herself as reactionary, meaning she responded to the instigation of her classmate and rarely inspired the fights. It is difficult to know if this was always the case, as she admitted that she had a bad attitude and temper, and was easily incited. These conflicts greatly impacted her ability to excel academically in school. When I asked her why she did not receive good grades she replied, "It was like 'cause I like let things get to me in the classroom. Like if this person say something to me, I kept an attitude and be ready to fight them and things like that. But it wasn't nothing cause of the work. It's because I let other people bother me."

Both Carmella and Buddha described severe social aggression from their female peers, which created hostile school environment. When social aggression impacts students in such a manner that they cannot concentrate on the academic aspects of school, school becomes an unsafe zone. Many students' response to a hostile school environment is to withdraw. One research report found that 1 in 12 students leave or stay away from the school environment due to fear of harassment (Stephens, 1996). Though Carmella and Buddha dropped out of school for a multitude of reasons, the conflict with their peers definitely was one of them.

Gender Equity in Special Education

Celina and Buddha described possible learning and behavioral disabilities. Celina often spoke of her inability to "pay attention" in class and how her mind would wander. Buddha described her verbal and physical conflicts with other students as occurring many times in a week. Yet, neither of these young women were referred for evaluation for special education services. This failure to acknowledge that these young women were in need of special education services is an oversight that happens to girls in the educational system; it stems from the gender bias that females face in society and in the classroom.

Teacher-student interaction research indicates that girls received less attention from teachers, were less academically challenged than boys, and when praised by teachers, were praised for social behaviors rather than academic accomplishment (Sadker & Sadker, 1994; Bogart, 1992; AAUW, 1991, 1992; Klein, 1985). Since girls as a whole receive less attention from teachers in the classroom, girls with disabilities receive even less attention. When correlating race to the amount of teacher attention received, researchers found that the order was: White males, minority males, White females, and minority females (Sadker & Sadker, 1994, p.50). African American females were the least likely to receive clear feedback that was of an academic nature (Phillips, 1998). Therefore, minority females receive the least amount of teacher attention. When the issue of disability is included, female disabled students are less attended when mainstreamed into the classroom and also in special education classrooms, with minority females ranking the lowest (Hansen & Smith, 2001).

Gender bias in teacher-student interaction is also translated into gender bias in referral for special education services, since teachers are also responsible for the referrals. In Kratovil and Bailey's (1986) literature review of special education and gender, they found that boys were referred for special education services more often and at an earlier age, and had less difficulty with receiving related support services once they were tracked for special education. Boys are overwhelmingly referred and admitted to special education services (Wehmeyer & Schwartz, 2001; Anderson, 1997; Andrews, Wisniewski, & Mulick, 1997; Reschly, 1996; Russo & Talbert-Johnson, 1997; Harmon, Stockton, & Contrucci, 1992). When studying the bias in referrals, Wehmeyer and Schwartz (2001) found that the primary basis for boys' referral to special education services was behavioral, though boys were in need of the services. If behavior is the main indicator for teachers' referrals, girls are at a disadvantage as they are socialized to behave more appropriately. Wehmeyer and Schwartz state, "The suggestion from these findings is that girls who are not as likely to be acting out are not likely to be referred for learning problems, thus they will have to experience more significant problems to gain the support they need" (2001, p. 278).

Celina's lack of a referral to special education services is explained by these findings, as she is both female and African American, two factors that indicate that she is least likely to receive teacher attention and referral for services. Also, she stated that she was always well-behaved in class, which means that she would not receive much of the teacher's attention. Buddha;

however, is an unusual case. She was very disruptive in class and frequently reprimanded by administrators for her behavior, yet she was not referred to special education services. If referrals are predominantly behaviorally based, the teachers' failure to refer her is evidence of the great gender bias in special education.

Socioeconomic Implications of Prostitution for African American Women

The socioeconomic implications of prostitution for African American women have not been sufficiently examined, even by Black feminists. While much attention is given to the sexual exploitation of Black women and the social implications of race and class that stem out of the legacy of slavery, African American women who work as prostitutes are not often addressed, as Patricia Hill Collins laments: "Perhaps the most curious omission has been the virtual silence of the Black feminist community concerning the participation of far too many Black women in prostitution. Ironically, while the image of African American women as prostitutes has been aggressively challenged, the reality of African American women who work as prostitutes remains unexplored...." (1990, p. 164). This is a costly oversight, as Black prostitutes are at the center of the race, class, and gender debate, and are more disenfranchised than African American women who are not prostitutes. If African American women rank last on the totem pole of society, the African American prostitute ranks even lower.

Historically, African American women's sexuality has been commodified, their value as slaves tied to their ability to bear children who would increase their slave master's workforce. Therefore, slave women did not have a right to their own bodies, as they were forced to breed children. At the same time, female slaves were the property of their owners and were often forced to be their concubines. As bell hooks (1981) points out, whereas prostitutes receive compensation for sex, slave women did not and were coerced. It was seen as their duty; they had no legal right to deny their masters since they were their chattel.

In the slavery era, Black women were domestic servants, working in the fields and houses of their masters. Once free, these women continued to serve in domestic labor roles for minimal pay. For a great part of the twentieth century, African American women continued to serve as maids, since employment options were limited. Even today, a great number of African American women work in the service industry. Because Black women face racial discrimination and inequality and less access to quality education, they have fewer opportunities for traditional work; therefore, they are forced to consider prostitution as an economic option more frequently than White women.

This lack of economic options contributed to Carmella's and Buddha's entrance into prostitution; Carmella did not have the financial means to provide basic needs to her infant son, and Buddha did not have the money to pay for an apartment for herself and her son. While there are fewer traditional work opportunities for people without education and job skills, there are even fewer for women of color.

Sexual Violence Against Women

and Psychological Denial of Tragedies

Research on the psychological backgrounds of adolescent prostitutes found that the majority of them have suffered some form of physical or mental abuse which may have indirectly predisposed them to prostitution. 65% report that rape was their first sexual encounter, 70% were emotionally abused, 60% were sexually abused (Schaffer & DeBlassie, 1984, p. 690), and 68% suffered psychological and emotional problems (Silbert & Pines, 1982, p.485). These statistics of sexual violence against women are of grave importance; the way in which abuse is addressed or not addressed has a great impact on these young women's entrance into prostitution.

All three participants suffered tragic experiences in their childhood and throughout their lives. Carmella and Celina were molested and physically abused, and Buddha was raped by young men she knew and abandoned by her mother and father. Carmella was devastated by the molestation, admitting that it altered the way she viewed herself and her relationship with men. "They taking it [sex] from you. I looked at it like, I know this is not the way it's supposed to be. When you say no, you say no and that stuck with me for many years, even now. It's still affecting me, with me, I still don't look at them the same...It took an effect on me. Cause it's like I didn't care."

Celina's maternal uncle molested her when she was seven years old and she never told anyone about it. The way she dealt with the trauma was to "push it to the back of her mind" as she tries "not to let things bother her too much," though she admits that it began to trouble her as she got older. This event had to be a key event in Celina's development. Researchers have found that, of young women who enter prostitution under the age of 20, 65% report that rape was their first sexual encounter (Ivers & Carlson, 1987). This mental blocking of tragedies is the same way that she dealt with the neglect and verbal abuse from her mother, and the domestic violence her father inflicted upon her mother.

Buddha was raped and told her grandmother and sister about it. Though they encouraged her to press charges because Buddha knew the young men, she never did. She told me that like Celina, she tried not to think about it or let it bother her. However, she was more vocal in addressing her traumatic issues, as she told her mother and father how she felt about their absences.

None of the participants received any counseling for these traumatic events for years. Instead, they tucked them away in a place deep inside. In fact, Carmella began counseling a year prior to my meeting her. Yet these events deeply colored the way in which they viewed themselves, others, and the world around them.

CHAPTER NINE

Conclusions

The seed for this intellectual journey was planted years ago, as I struggled to understand the reasons why Elisha, one of my most brilliant students, left my classroom for the street corner, leading life as a prostitute. At the time, I did not know what to do, so I did nothing. Time passed and she faded into the recesses of my mind. Though I was deeply concerned about her, I thought of her as an anomaly and did not consider that many more teenage girls were living Elisha's reality. One year later, during a 12-hour patrol with a police officer, I stared into the faces of more than 20 teenage girls, who were street prostitutes. So many questions burned in my mind, yet I did not ask any; I simply observed in an awe-struck silence. Those questions never left me, and what began as a 20-page inquiry into what I learned was an epidemic has grown into this document. Though I have not found answers to my questions, I have begun to understand the life experiences, education, and schooling of these young women.

This study included three young women, ages 18, 24, and 25. The backgrounds of the participants were varied: two were raised by grandparents in households with extended family members, while one lived in a two-parent household with her siblings. Their economic backgrounds also varied; Celina's family was middle-income, while Carmella and Buddha's families lived below the poverty level (in Carmella's case, her family became involved with the drug industry to escape this poverty). All of the women had different backgrounds, were involved in prostitution for different reasons, and were immersed in different forms of prostitution (street prostitution, independent prostitution, and survival sex). And yet, even though each of the participants attended different schools, their in-school educational experiences were similar and they also share some of the same life experiences.

My primary reason for undertaking this study was to understand how and why some female adolescent dropouts transition into prostitution. Upon the initial literature review, I found that most adolescent prostitutes are dropouts, which led me to their in-school educational experiences. Further review of literature indicated that these young women are products of dysfunctional environments (Ellenwood, 1991; Chesney-Lind, 1989; Figueria-McDonough, 1985; Weisberg, 1985; Ivers & Carlson, 1987; Bracey, 1983). Therefore, in order to gain a full understanding of their educational experiences, I examined their in-school and nonschool educational experiences, as the two merged. These women's in-school and nonschool experiences consisted of their in-class experiences, home environment, community, family, and peers. Their nonschool experiences permeated the boundaries of their in-school experiences.

This study was designed to give voice to these young women, whose voices are absent from many reports about their lives. The oral histories, coupled with the literature on female dropouts, adolescent prostitutes, and feminist and womanist theory provide the basis for the analysis and a lens through which I have attempted to make meaning of their educational experiences, both in-school and out-of-school.

Though each case study presented themes that were particular to the participant (as they were addressed in the microanalysis at the end of each case study), there were five themes that were present across the case studies.

The first theme, *the disconnection between the school and the community*, confirmed that their in-school curriculum rarely addressed the issues that they faced in their community and home environment. All of the participants lived in communities that faced socioeconomic challenges; however, their teachers did not address these issues. As a result, their in-school experiences took place in a vacuum, without any acknowledgment of the realities of their life. Therefore, the participants viewed their in-school and nonschool experiences as separate. It was difficult for women to understand how what they were learning in school affected them in any "real world" way. To them, school became artificial and boring for them.

The second theme, *teachers as "othermothers,"* emerged out of the participants' close relationships with at least one of their teachers. Since all of the women lived in households where they lacked supervision and attention, there was a need for guidance from an adult. In all of their cases, that adult was a female teacher. They went to these teachers with their personal problems, and many times the interaction took place after school hours or during a time other than class time. In Celina's case, she spent the weekend at the teacher's house. These teachers seemed to take a communal approach to raising children, as they extended their responsibility for these students beyond their classroom obligations. Each participant stated that they were greatly impacted by these teachers' presence and likened their relationships to that of mothers and daughters.

The third theme, *social aggression among schoolgirls,* grew out of the negative and combative experiences the participants had with female classmates. All of the women stated that they did not have close friends at school. If they did have friends at school, they were family members. In the cases of Carmella and Buddha, the rivalry with female classmates resulted in frequent fights. Carmella suffered abuse from female peers from elementary school through high school. At times, she was attacked by groups of girls. The tension with female classmates greatly affected their social experiences at school, and made it less difficult to drop out as they were socially rejected and taunted. Buddha was involved in conflicts with female classmates on a daily basis. The conflicts were often verbal, but at times they were physical.

Buddha and Celina both struggled with what could have been disabilities, such as attention deficit disorder and behavioral disorder; however, neither woman was referred to special education services for an evaluation. In Buddha's case, her behavior was evident, as she described fighting on a daily basis. In spite of her outbursts, brawls, and suspensions, she was not evaluated. Celina's attention deficit disorder may have been less evident, as she was able to fade into the backdrop of the classroom. However, the failure of the teachers to refer them for special education evaluation and services speaks to the fact that issues with *gender equity in special education* remain, as girls are referred to special education services far less than boys (Wehmeyer & Schwartz, 2001; Anderson, 1997; Andrews, Wisniewski & Mulick, 1997; Reschly 1996; Russo & Talbert-Johnson, 1997; Harmon, Stockton, & Contrucci, 1992).

When asked if they thought education was important, each of the participants affirmed that it was; however, only Carmella had returned to school to obtain a G.E.D. They described how a lack of education affected their ability to obtain gainful employment and viewed this lack as a barrier. For many reasons, education appeared to be regarded as something that was out of reach. As Celina stated, she could not "plan" to get a G.E.D. Buddha repeatedly stated that she needed to return to school and was in the process of trying when I met her. Though all participants stated that education was important, they all had difficulty completing a G.E.D.

I asked all of the women if they thought that education was important and why. They all agreed that it was important because it provided the preparation needed to secure a job; however, their actions regarding their schooling did not reflect this importance. As I stated earlier, Celina never actually committed to or followed through with a G.E.D. course; and though Buddha dropped out when she was 14 years old, she only attempted to enroll in the G.E.D. at the time we met. Carmella's commitment to her education was more evident, as she had completed her G.E.D. and had enrolled in a job-training program which provides skills for entry-level secretarial work and job placement. Though Carmella told me that she aspires to become a counselor for women who are struggling with prostitution and drug addiction, she has not taken any steps towards enrolling in college to pursue a degree in counseling. Although I believe that the women's regard for education was sincere, they seemed to lack the follow-through and commitment needed to continue their education.

Carmella and Buddha were suffering economic hardship when they started prostituting. Carmella was unemployed and living with her boyfriend when her infant son needed milk and diapers. When her boyfriend suggested that she become a prostitute to earn the money she needed to provide care for her son, she was in such a position of need that she agreed. When Buddha came to an impasse with her grandmother and she and her son had to leave home, she did not have any place to go. As a result, she went to the man who agreed to provide shelter in exchange for sex. Fearing homelessness, she agreed so that she and her son would not have to live on the streets. While these cases raise the issue of the *socioeconomic implications of prostitution for African American women*, this theme has been of issue for African American women throughout history, from the slavery era to the present day.

Research on the rates of abuse on prostitutes indicates that 60% of prostitutes were sexually abused as children and 84% were raped (Silbert & Pines, 1982). All of the women in this study were victims of sexual violence. Carmella and Celina were both molested as children, while Buddha was gang-raped, hence, the *sexual violence against females* theme. Carmella's molestation was devastating to her self-esteem and her opinion of men and intimate relationships. She was adamant about her distrust of men and went as far as to say that she believed that she would have remained a virgin had it not been for the molestation. Though she worked in the prostitution industry, she professed that she did not enjoy having sexual relations with her clients or her "husbands." Based on her assertion that she would not be sexually active were she not molested, I gathered that the molestation played a huge part in her transition to prostitute, as it left her broken and sexually disconnected from her body.

Celina was also molested by her maternal uncle as a child. Though she stated that she "pushed it out of her mind" and never told anyone besides me about it, she admitted that it troubles her a great deal now that she is an adult. Unlike Carmella, Celina does not draw a connection between the molestation and prostitution; however, it likely had an effect on her sexual behavior.

The sexual violence that African American women have suffered from the time of slavery until the present day is tremendous, and the rate of sexual abuse is exacerbated for women within the prostitution industry; 96% of prostitutes are raped within the context of their work (Silbert & Pines, 1982). In a case that Buddha mentioned, the sexual crimes extended beyond rape to murder, as she referred to the case of the serial killer in her neighborhood killing prostitutes. This killing of prostitutes is actually quite common, and their murders often go unsolved, since police are less likely to diligently seek their killers due to the dangerous nature of their work. Also, many prostitutes are not closely connected to their families; therefore, the families are less likely to demand that the police perform an in-depth investigation.

All of the participants in the study had suffered severe tragedies in the course of their lives. Carmella and Celina had been molested as children and Buddha had been raped. Both Carmella and Celina had been victims of domestic violence. Celina was reared in a household in which physical confrontations between her parents were the norm, and she described her mother as mentally and verbally abusive. The father of Celina's son had been murdered prior to the child's birth. In spite of all of these events, which have devastating psychological effects, none of the women received psychological counseling until years later. In fact, Carmella was the only participant who received any counseling, and she began the sessions the year before we met. Celina told me during one of her interviews that she had "pushed" all of those things out of her mind and had only thought deeply about them since we began our interviews. On numerous occasions the women told me that they tried not to let things "bother" them. In order to function, they simply did not address these traumatic occurrences because they were not able to process them. This inability to address these events led to the *psychological denial of tragedies* theme. One specific example is Celina's mother's drinking. Celina shared with me that her mother used to drink everyday until she was incoherent. She stated that her mother had stopped drinking as much, though the benchmark for her mother's improvement was that she only drank a fifth of liquor a day now. This would be deemed as alcoholism, though when asked Celina stated that her mother was not an alcoholic. Though people often block out events that are too traumatic for them to process, denial of those tragic events can lead to self-destructive behavior.

Though the participants in this study have different backgrounds, come from different family structures, and practiced different forms of prostitution, there are many similarities in their in-school and nonschool experiences, which led to the emergence of eight themes. Issues that were common to all three participants were: teachers as mentors, teenage pregnancy, lack of parental supervision, unstable home environments, truancy, sexual abuse, crime-laden communities, and drug use. Issues that were common to at least two participants were: unevaluated and undiagnosed special needs, boredom with school, disdain for certain school subjects, conflicts with peers (particularly females), financial crisis, and domestic abuse.

Recommendations

Based on the themes that emerged in this study, there are several recommendations for addressing the needs of young women who have dropped out or are on the fringes of dropping out. It is recommended that the following structures be put in place:

Special Education Services for Girls

Teachers must be aware of girls who exhibit the need for special education services. There is a gender bias in tracking for special education services, as boys are the primary recipients of these services (Wehmeyer & Schwartz, 2001; Anderson, 1997; Andrews, Wisniewski, & Mulick, 1997; Reschly, 1996; Russo & Talbert-Johnson, 1997; Harmon, Stockton, & Contrucci, 1992). Two of the three participants in this study described behavior that needed to be evaluated for special education referrals, such as attention deficit disorder and behavior disorder. Teachers are less likely to notice when girls are not participatory in class or not attentive, as they are quiet and fitting into the stereotypical female gender role. Teachers must be more attentive to girls, since many may be exhibiting signs of learning disorders.

Negotiated Curriculum and Authentic Learning

Student-centered classrooms, negotiated curriculum, and authentic learning are critical to students' success in school. Two participants in this study stated that many times they were bored in some classes in school and would often cut these classes. One stated that she would offer her opinion on what she thought they should learn, but it was not implemented in the curriculum. When students feel that the curriculum is not relevant to their lives and do not understand why they need to learn the content, they divest and begin to see schooling as irrelevant. If students have a voice in their curriculum and it is negotiated between the teachers and students, they are more likely to be vested in their learning.

Teachers as Othermothers

Teachers are sometimes the only adult that students feel like they can trust and depend on. When students are considering dropping out due to nonschool or in-school curricula, teachers with whom they have a personal connection can be their only incentive for remaining in the school environment. While mentoring programs with outside community members are good, girls on cusp of dropping out need daily interaction with someone who they respect and trust. The teachers lend a sense of support and guidance, and act as a sounding board for many very important and potentially life-altering decisions. When a personal relationship with a teachers is forged which extends to conversations about life in general, students are less likely to drop out.

Mentoring and Support Groups

Mentoring and support groups for girls in schools that are not sports-related or targeted to pregnant girls are needed, as many girls who dropped out are socially isolated prior to leaving the school environment. Those who are not active in school sports still need to feel a part of the school environment and need a safe place to receive positive reinforcement and support. All of the three participants in this study stated that they had female teachers who served in this role. Also, while all of the participants in this study were teenage mothers, research indicates that only 40% of female dropouts withdraw due to pregnancy (Jordan et al., 1994). A support group would be instrumental in identifying and addressing both the academic and personal needs of these girls.

Conflict Resolution Especially for Girls

A task force or group must be in place to deal with conflict resolution among schoolgirls. Two of the three participants were constantly involved in conflict with their female classmates. Some of these conflicts were verbal and steeped in emotional intimidation, which stemmed from jealousy and other social issues, and often escalated to physical confrontations. As a result, the participants were constantly fighting, and these social dynamics had a great impact on their in-school experience. A task force on relations between girls is warranted, as it would teach girls how to exist peacefully. The issue of social aggression among girls has become more serious in recent years and seems to be escalating (Wiseman, 2003; Eisner, 2002; Flanigan, 2002; Simmons, 2002; Vail, 2002; Artz, 1997); as such, schools must begin to address it in the same way that they are beginning to address school violence resulting from social alienation among boys.

Relationships between the School and the Community

Stronger connections must be made between schools and their surrounding communities. Many schools are disconnected from the issues that are prevalent in the communities in which they are located. By being ignorant of these issues or not addressing them, students become casualties of their environment. These issues need to be addressed, and schools need to create programs that function as community outreach and a means by which to get community members vested in what takes place within the school.

Extracurricular Activities

Girls should be encouraged to participate in extracurricular activities. Extracurricular activities provide a positive adult relationship with at least one person who may serve as a role model for the teacher. Coaches are often the first adults in which students confide, and they can offer direction to services for students. Also, extracurricular activities provide an opportunity for personal growth and are effective in improving self-esteem. It can also create a sense of belonging in the school environment.

Counseling Services

Stronger in-school counseling services that can refer girls to outside counseling if necessary are a must for girls on the fringes of dropping out. Though many of the young women in this study faced traumatic life events, only one stated that she received in-school counseling. Though many of the issues these women faced were too severe for an in-school guidance counselor to address, they could have referred these students to outside resources. Such service is necessary for these young women to address and overcome their issues.

Notes

Preface

1   This lack of earning power is related to their lack of basic educational credentials such as a high school diploma or G.E.D.

2   Silbert and Pines report that 81% were not attending school at the time of their first prostitution experience. Enablers reports that 40% were not in school and that 20% attended sometimes but were truant.

3   Feminist researchers do not agree that feminist research methodology must be limited to females only; this remains to be a topic of debate.

Chapter One

4   Jordan et al., 1994 found that the top reasons for dropping out for females were (1) school-related (push out factors): 31% (2) family related (pull-out factors): 15% (3) job-related factors: 12%. All of these indicators were compounded for girls who are of low SES and minority status.

5   Baca et al. (1989) state that 77% of their female dropout subjects cite reasons other than pregnancy for leaving school.

6   Silbert & Pines (1982) report a dropout rate of 81%, Enablers (1978) report a 40% dropout rate and 20% truancy.

7   This figure includes data on participants who were adults at the time of the studies describing their past experiences as adolescent prostitutes, as well as those who were currently adolescents.

Chapter Two

8   "Education" is used widely here in the sense of life education; more traditional forms of education such as those leading to diplomas and degree will be referred to as "schooling".

9   Some drop out at the elementary level whereas others may drop out high school level.

10   See Allen, D. on "Young Male Prostitutes" and URSA for bibliography on Adolescent Male and Female Prost.

11   See Collins (1990), hooks (1984), and Lorde (1984) for discussion of Black women and "otherness".

12   For Walker's complete definition of womanism, see the appendix.

13   For a more complete discussion of womanism as encompassing all people of color, see
      Katie G. Cannon's "Black Womanist Ethics."

Chapter Three

14   Nonschool curriculum refers to that which is learned outside of the school environment,
      from sources such as home, community, peers, media, etc.

Chapter Six

15   Sibert & Pines' (1984) study of 200 young women revealed 18% enter for adventure and
      glamour.

References

Alexander, P. (1987). Prostitution: A difficult issue for feminists. In F. Delacoste & P. Alexander (Eds.), *Sex work: Writings by women in the sex industry* (184-214). Pittsburgh: Cleis.

Allen, D. (1980). Young male prostitutes: A psychosocial study. *Archives of Sexual Behavior, 9*(5), 399-426.

American Association of University Women (AAUW). (1991). *Shortchanging girls, shortchanging America.* Washington D.C.,Author.

American Association of University Women (AAUW). (1992*) How schools shortchange girls: A study of major findings on girls and education.* Washington, D.C., Author.

Anderson, E. (1990). *Streetwise : Race, class and change in an urban community.* Chicago: University of Chicago Press.

Anyon, J. (1996). Social class and the hidden curriculum of work. In E. Hollins (Ed.), *Transforming curriculum for a culturally diverse society* (179-203). Mahwah, NJ: Lawrence Earlbaum Associates.

Ansariyah-Grace, T. (1995). Urbanisation and the beauty myth. *Southern African Feminist Review, 1*(2), 99-110.

Artz, S.T.G. (1997). *The life worlds and practices of violent school girls.* Unpublished doctoral dissertation. University of Victoria.

Asante, M.K. (1987). *The Afrocentric idea.* Philadelphia: Temple University Press.

American Association of University Women. (1992). *Shortchanging girls, shortchanging America.* Washington D.C.: American Association of University Women.

Anderson, K. (1997). Gender bias and special education referrals. *Annals of Dyslexia, 47,* 151-62.

Andrews, T., Wisniewski, J., and Mulick A. (1997). Variables influencing teachers' decisions to refer children for school psychological assessment services, *Psychology in the Schools, 34*(3), 239-44.

Baca, C. C. et al. (1989). *Women at risk project: Dropout factors study.* San Diego: San Diego City Schools, CA. Community Relations and Integration Services Division.

Banks, J. A. & Banks, C. (1995). *Handbook of research on multicultural education.* New York: Macmillan.

Banks, J. A. & Banks, C. (1998). *Handbook of research on multicultural education.* New York: Macmillan.

Banks, R. (1997). *Bullying in schools.* Champaign, IL: Clearinghouse on Elementary and Early Childhood Education. (ERIC Document Reproduction Service No. ED407154)

Baron, S. (2001). Street youth labour market experiences and crime. *The Canadian Review of Sociology and Anthropology, 38*(2), 189-215.

Barry, K. (1979). *Female sexual slavery.* Englewood Cliffs, NJ: Prentice-Hall.

Belenky, M., Clinchy, B., Goldberger, N., & Tarule, J. (1986). *Women's ways of knowing: The development of self, voice and mind.* New York: Basic Books.

Bell, L. (Ed.). (1987). *Good girls, bad girls.* Seattle: Seal.

Bogart, K. (1992). *Solutions that work: Identification and elimination of barriers to the participation of female and minority students in academic educational programs* (Vols. 1-3). Washington, D.C.: National Educational Association.

Bowker, A. (1993). *Sister in the blood: The education of women in native America.* Newton, MA: WEEA Resource Center/EDC.

Boyd, J. (1994). *In the company of my sisters: Black women and self esteem.* New York: Penguin.

Boyer, D. (1982). Easy money: Adolescent involvement in prostitution. In S. Davidson (Ed.), *Justice for young women: Close up on critical issues* (73-97). Tucson, AZ: New Directions for Young Women.

Boyer, D. (1993). *Survival sex in King County, helping women out.* Seattle: Women's Advisory Board.

Boykin, A. W. (1994). Afrocultural expression and its implications for schooling. In E. Hollins (Ed.), *Teaching diverse populations: Formulating a knowledge base* (.pp.243-274). New York: SUNY.

Boykin, A. W. (2001). The challenges of cultural socialization in the schooling of African-American elementary school children: Exposing the hidden curriculum. In W.H. Watkins, J.H. Lewis, & V. Chou (Eds.), *Race and education: The roles of history and society in education African American students* (pp.190-199). Needham Heights, MA: Allyn & Bacon.

Bracey, D. (1982). "Concurrent and consecutive abuse: The juvenile prostitute". In B. Price and N. Sokoloff (Eds.), *Women and the criminal justice system.* New York: Clark, Broadman, and Co.

Bracey, D. (1983). The juvenile prostitute: Victim and offender. Second international proceedings on victimology: International perspectives. *Victimology, 8*(3-4), 151-160.

Brock, D. R. (1998). *Making work, making trouble: Prostitution as a social problem.* Toronto: University of Toronto Press.

Brown, M. (1979). Teenage prostitution. *Adolescence, 14* (56), 555-679.

Burke, C. G. (1978). Report form Paris: Women's writing and the women's movement. *Signs: Journal of Women in Culture and Society, 3*, 843-855.

Calhoun, G., Jurgens, J., & Chen, F. (1993). The neophyte female delinquent: A review of the literature. *Adolescence, 28*(110), 461-71.

Caplan G. M. (1984). The facts of life about teenage prostitution. *Delinquency, 30*(1), 69-74.

Carroll, B. (1976). *Liberating women's history: Theoretical and critical essays.* Chicago: University of Illinois Press, 1976.

Cervantes, L. (1965). *The dropout: Causes and cures.* Ann Arbor: University of Michigan Press.

Chesney-Lind, M. (1989). The juvenile prostitute: Victim and offender. *Victimology, 8,* 151-60.

Clardy, P., Robinson, C., O'C. Jones,T. & Michie, G. (2001). *Investigation of critical issues in curriculum through documentary.* Paper presented at AERA Seattle, WA 2001. (ERIC Document Reproduction Service No. ED452264)

Cohen, L. and Manion, L (1989). *Research methods in education.* New York: Routledge.

Cole, S. (1987). Sexual politics: Contradictions and explosions. In L. Bell (Ed.), *Good girls, bad girls* (pp.33-36). Seattle: Seal Press.

Cole, A. (1994, April). *Doing life history research in theory and in practice*. Paper prepared at the annual meeting of the American Educational Research Association, New Orleans, LA.

Collins, P. (1990). *Black feminist thought: Knowledge, consciousness and the politics of empowerment*. New York: Routledge.

Combahee River Collective. (1986). *The Combahee River collective: Black feminists organizing in the seventies and eighties*. Albany: NY: Kitchen Table: Women of Color Press.

Creswell, J. W. (1998). *Qualitative inquiry and research design: Choosing among five traditions*. Thousand Oaks, CA: Sage.

Deisher, R., Robinson, G., & Boyer, D. (1982). The adolescent female and male prostitute. *Pediatric Annals, 11*(10), 819-25.

Delpit, L. (1995). *Other people's children: Cultural conflict in the classroom*. New York: The New Press.

Denzin, N. K. (1989). *Interpretive biography*. Newbury Park, CA: Sage.

Dewey, J. (1916). *Democracy and education*. New York: Free Press.

Dizon, N. Z. (2003). High school students suspended for hazing. *The Associated Press News Service*, May 13, 2003. http://www.ap.org (accessed June 6, 2003).

Dowdell, J.B. (1996). *The dilemma of dealing with the Black male dropout problem*. Unpublished doctoral dissertation. Ann Arbor: University of Michigan.

Dubois, W. E. B. (1903). *The souls of black folk*. Penguin: New York.

Dworkin, A. (1987). *Intercourse*. New York: Free Press.

Earle, J. & Roach, V. (1989). *Female dropouts: A new perspective*. Newton, MA: WEEA Publishing Center.

Education Development Center, Inc. (1990, March). Female dropouts: The challenge. Newton, MA: *WEEA Publishing Center Digest*.

Eisner, E. (1979). Social influences on educational practice. *Instructor, 88*(8), 28-32.

Eisner, J. (2002). Books look at 'woman's inhumanity to woman' from girls on up. *The Philadelphia inquirer*, March 29, 2002. http://www.philly.com/mld/inquirer/ (accessed June 6, 2003).

Ellenwood, A. et al. (1991, April). *Runaway: A silent crisis*. Paper presented at the National Conference on Troubled Adolescents at Milwaukee, WI.

Enablers. (1978). *Juvenile prostitution in Minnesota: The report of a research project*. St. Paul, MN: The Enablers.

Evans, G. (1988). Those Loud Black Girls. In D. Spender and E. Sarah (Eds.), *Learning to lose: Sexism and education*. London: The Women's Press.

Evans, J. (1995). *Feminist theory today: An introduction to second-wave feminism*. London: Sage.

Figueiria-McDonough, J. (1985). Are girls different? Gender discrepancies between delinquent behavior and control. *Child Welfare, 64*, 273-288.

Fine, M. (1986). *Framing dropouts: Notes on the politics of an urban public high school*. Albany, NY: SUNY Press.

Fine, M. (1986). Why urban adolescents drop into and out of high school. *Teachers College Record, 87*, 393-409.

Fine, M. (1992). *Disruptive voices: The possibilities of feminist research*. Ann Arbor: University of

Michigan Press.

Fine, M. and Zane, N. (1989). On being' wrapped tight: When low income females drop out of high school. In L. Weiss (Ed.), *Dropouts in schools: Issues, dilemmas, solution*. Albany, NY: SUNY Press.

Fisher, B. et al. (1982). *Juvenile prostitution: A resource manual*. San Francisco: URSA.

Flanigan, K. (2002). Stinging cruelty: Aggression by girls gets fresh attention. *Milwaukee Journal Sentinel*, June 25, 2002. http://www.jsonline.com/ (accessed June 5, 2003).

Fordham, S. (1988). Racelessness as a factor in Black students' school success: Pragmatic strategy or pyrrhic victory? *Harvard Educational Review, 58*, 54-84.

Fordham, S. (1993). "Those loud Black girls": (Black) women, silence, and gender "passing" in the academy. *Anthropology and Education Quarterly, 24* (1), 3-32.

Fordham, S. & Ogbu, J. (1986). Black students' school success: Coping with the burden of "acting white." *The Urban Review, 18,* 176-206.

Foster, M. (1995). African American teachers and culturally relevant pedagogy. In J.A. Banks & C.M. Banks (Eds.), *Handbook of research on multicultural education* (pp. 570 – 581). New York: Macmillan.

Freire, Paulo. (1998). *Pedagogy of the oppressed*. New York: Continuum.

Garcia, M.T. (1994). Border culture. In R. Takaki (Ed.), *From different shores: Perspectives on race and ethnicity in America* (pp. 72-81). New York: Oxford University Press.

Giroux, H. (1992). *Border crossings: Cultural workers and the politics of education*. New York: Routledge.

Gonzalez, N. et al. (1993). *Teacher research on the funds of knowledge: Learning from households*. (Report No. BBB29304). Santa Cruz, CA: National Center for Research on Cultural Diversity and Second Language Learning. (ERIC Document Reproduction Service No. ED360825)

Gray, D. (1973). Turning-out: A study of teenage prostitution. *Urban Life and Culture,* (4), 401-425.

Grayson, D. R. (1995). Is it fake? Black women's hair as spectacle and spec(tac)ular. *Camera Obscura: Feminism, Culture, and Media studies*, 36, 13-29.

Greene, J. M. (1999). Prevalence and correlates of survival sex among runaway and homeless youth. *American Journal of Public Health, 89*(9), 1406-1410.

Guidroz, K. (1996). "I'm more than my private parts.". *Off Our Backs,21*(6), 8-18.

Hallstein, D. (2000). Where standpoint stands now: An introduction and commentary. *Women's Studies in Communication, 23*(1), 1-15.

Hanson, K. & Smith, S. (2001). Gender equity in education: Change and challenge. In H. Rousso and M. Wehmeyer (Eds.), *Double jeopardy: Addressing gender equity in special education* (pp. 59-94). Albany, NY : SUNY Press.

Harmon, J. Stockton, S. & Contrucci, C. (1992). *Gender disparities in special education* (Report No. 143). Madison, WI: Bureau for Exceptional Children, Wisconsin Department of Public Instruction. (ERIC Document Reproduction Service No. ED358631).

Harstock, N. (1990). Postmodernism and political change: Issues for feminist theory. *Cultural Critique, 14*, 15-33.

Henry, A. (1998). 'Invisible and 'womanish': Black girls negotiating their lives in an African-centered school in the USA. *Race, Ethnicity, and Education, 1*(2), 151-170.

Hilliard, A. (1995). *The maroon within us: Selected essays on African American community socialization.* Baltimore: Black Classic Press.

Hilliard, A. (2001). "Race," identity, hegemony, and education: What do we need to know now? In W.H. Watkins, J.H. Lewis, & V. Chou (Eds.), *Race and education: The roles of history and society in education African American students* (pp.7-25). Needham Heights, MA: Allyn & Bacon.

Hirschmann, N. J. (1997). Feminist standpoint as postmodern strategy. *Women & Politics, 18*(3), 73-92.

hooks, b. (1981). *Ain't I a woman: Black women and feminism.* Boston: South End Press

hooks, b. (1984). *Feminist theory: From margins to center.* Boston: South End Press.

hooks, b. (1989). *Talking back: Thinking feminist, thinking black.* Boston: South End Press.

Horgan, D. (1995). *Achieving gender equity: Strategies for the classroom.* Boston: Allyn and Bacon.

Illinois Workforce Advantage (2003). Facts about Chicago. Retrieved, June 6, 2003 from http://www.illinois.gov/iwa

Ivers, K. & Carlson, H. (1987, August-September). *Needs assessment of female street kids: Children in danger.* Paper presented at the Annual Convention of the American Psychological Association.

Jackman, N. R. et al. (1963). The self-image of the prostitute. *Sociological Quarterly, 2,* 150-161.

Jaggar, A. (1991). Prostitution. In A. Soble (Ed.), *Philosophy of sex: Contemporary readings.* Savage, MD: Rowman & Littlefield.

James, J. (1980). *Entrance into juvenile prostitution.* Final report submitted to the National Institute of Mental Health, August, 1980.

James, J. & Meyerling, J. (1977). Early sexual experience and prostitution. *American Journal of Psychiatry, 134,* 1381-85.

Jenness, V. (1993). *Making it work: The prostitutes' rights movement in perspective.* New York: Aldine De Gruyter.

Johnson, J. J. (1992). *Teen prostitution.* New York: Franklin Watts.

Jordan, W. J. et al. (1994). *Exploring the complexity of early dropout causal structures.* Wasington, D.C.: Office of Educational Research and Improvement.

Joseph, G.L. & Lewis, J. (1981). *Common differences: Conflicts and black and white feminist perspectives.* Garden City, N.Y.: Anchor Press.

Kaufman, P., Kwon, J., Klein, S., & Chapman, C. (2000). Dropout rates in the United States: 1998. *Education Statistics Quarterly., 2*(1).

Klein, S. (1985). *Handbook for achieving sex equity through education.* Baltimore, MD: John Hopkins University Press.

Kratovil, J. and Bailey, S. (1986). Sex equity and disabled students. *Theory into Practice, 25,* 250-56.

Ladson-Billings, G. (1994). *The dreamkeepers: Successful teaching for African-American students.* San Francisco: Jossey-Bass.

Ladson-Billings, G. (1998). Toward a theory of culturally relevant pedagogy. In L. E. Beyer & M.

W. Apple (Eds.), *The curriculum: Problems, politics, and possibilities.* Albany, NY: SUNY Press.

Lather, P. (1991). *Feminist research and pedagogy with the postmodern.* New York: Routledge.

Lincoln, Y. and Denzin, N. (1994). The fifth moment. In N. Denzin and Y. Lincoln (Eds.), *Handbook of qualitative research* (pp. 575-586). Thousand Oaks, CA: Sage.

Liston, D.P. & Zeichner, K.M. (1996). *Culture and teaching.* Mahwah, NJ: Lawrence Erlbaum Associates.

Lorde, A. (1984). *Sister outsider.* Trumansberg, NY: Crossing.

Loury, A.K. (2002). West side residents battle drug war. *The Chicago Reporter.*, May 2002. http://www.chicagoreporter.com/2002/5-2002/recidivism/recidivism.htm (accessed June 5, 2003).

MacKinnon, C. A. (1987). *Feminism unmodified: Discourses on law and life.* Cambridge: Harvard University Press.

MacKinnon, C. A. (1983). Feminism, Marxism, method, and the state: Toward a feminist jurisprudence. *Signs, 8,* 635-639.

MacLeod, J. (1987). *Ain't no makin it.* Boulder, CO: Westview Press.

MacVicar, K. & Dillion, M. (1980). Childhood and adolescent development of ten prostitutes. *Journal of American Academy of Child Psychiatry, 19,* 14-59.

Maher, F. et al. (2001). *The feminist classroom: Dynamics of gender, race, and privilege.* Lanham, MD: Rowman and Littlefield.

Mannion, A. (1996). Profile: Humboldt Park. *Chicago Tribune,* May 6, 1996. http://www.chicagotribune.com (accesssed June 5, 2003).

Marx, K. (1975). *The economic and philosophical manuscripts, Karl Marx: Early writings* (R. Livingstone & G. Benton, Trans.) New York: Vintage.

Mays, J . (1980). The impact of neighbourhood values. In M. Craft, J. Raynor, & L. Cohen (Eds.), *Linking home and school* (pp. 56-69). London: Harper & Row Publishers.

McClintock, A. (1992). Screwing the system: Sex work, race and the law. *Boundary 2* (19), 70-95.

McCormick, T. (1994). *Creating the nonsexist classroom: A multicultural approach.* New York: Teachers College Press.

Mertl, S. (2001). Teen's killer loses appeal. *Toronto Star,* November 30, 2001. http://www.thestar.com (accessed June 6, 2003).

Michie, G. (1999). *Holler if you hear me: The education of a teacher and his students.* New York: Teachers College Press.

Miller, J. P. (1993). *The holistic curriculum.* Ontario: Oise Press.

Mungo, J. W. (1992). *The attitudes of school personnel toward potential black male dropouts.* Unpublished doctoral dissertation. Norfolk State University.

Nagle, J. (1997). *Whores and other feminists.* New York: Routledge.

Ngan-Ling Chow, E. (1994). The feminist movement: Where are all the Asian American women? In R Takaki (Ed.), *From different shores: Perspectives on race and ethnicity in America* (pp. 184-91). New York: Oxford University Press.

Ogbu, J. (1978). *Minority education and caste: The American system in cross-cultural perspective.* New York:

Academic Press.

Ogbu, J. (1995). Understanding cultural diversity and learning. In J. A. Banks & C. A. Banks (Eds.), *Handbook of Multicultural Education* (pp. 582-593). New York: Macmillan.

Omolade, B. (1994). *The rising song of African-American women.* New York: Routledge.

Overall, C. (1992). What's wrong with prostitution? Evaluating sex work. *Journal of Women in Culture and Society, 17,* 705-725.

Padilla, F.M. (1992). *The gang as an American enterprise.* New Brunswick, NJ: Rutgers University Press.

Palmer, P. M. (1994). White women/Black women: The dualism of female identity and experience. In R. Takaki (Ed.), *From different shores: Perspectives on race and ethnicity in America* (pp. 167-74). New York: Oxford University Press.

Pateman C. (1988). *The sexual contract.* Palo Alto, CA: Stanford University Press.

Pheterson, G. (Ed.) (1989). *A vindication of the rights of whores.* Seattle: Seal Press.

Phillips, L. (1998). *The girls report: What we know and need to know about growing up female.* New York: National Council for Research on Women.

Reinharz, S. (1992). *Feminist methods in social research.* New York: Oxford University Press.

Reschly, S. (1996). Identification and assessment of students with disabilities, *The Future of Children, 6*(1), 40-53.

Riger, S. (1992). Epistemological debates, feminist voices. *American Psychological, 47,* 730-740.

Ristock, J. L. & Pennel, J. (1996). *Community research as empowerment: Feminist links, postmodern interruptions.* Oxford, UK: Oxford University Press.

Romo-Carmona, M. (1987). *Companeras: Latina lesbian.* New York City: Latina Lesbian Project.

Rubin, G. (1984). Thinking sex: Notes for a radical theory on the politics of sexuality. In B. Vance (Ed.), *Pleasure and danger: Exploring female sexuality* (pp.267-319). London: Routledge Kegan Paul.

Rumberger, R. W. (1983). Dropping out of high school: The influences of race, sex, and family background. *American Educational Research Journal,* 20, 199-220.

Russell, D. E. H. (1993). *Against pornography: The evidence of harm.* Berkeley: Russell Publications.

Russo, C. & Talbert-Johnson, C. (1997). The overrepresentation of African American children in special education: Resegreation of educational programming? *Education and Urban Society, 29*(2), 136-48.

Sadker, M. & Sadker, D. (1994). *Failing at fairness: How America's schools cheat girls.* New York: Charles Scribner's Sons.

Sadker, M. & Sadker, D. (1995). *Failing at fairness: How our schools cheat girls.* New York: Touchstone.

Schaffer, B. & DeBlassie, R. (1984). Adolescent prostitution. *Adolescence, 19*(75), 689-696.

Schubert, W. H. (1981). Knowledge about out-of-school curriculum. *The Educational Forum,* 45(2), 185-199.

Schubert, W. H. (1986). *Curriculum: Perspective, paradigm, and possibility.* New York: Macmillan Publishing Company.

Schulman, L. S. (1997). The nature of disciplined inquiry in education. In R. M. Jaeger (Ed.), *Complementary methods for research in education* (pp. 1-70). Washington, D.C.: AERA.

Seng, M. J. (1989). Child sexual abuse and adolescent prostitution: A comparative analysis. *Adolescence, 24*(95), 665-675.

Sewell, T., Palmo, A., & Manni, J. (1981). High school dropout: Psychological, academic and vocational factors. *Urban Education, 16*, 65-76.

Shakeshaft, C., Mandel, L., Johnson, Y. & Wenk, A. (1998, April). *Transitions into middle middle school: The harassing nature of adolescent culture.* Paper presented at AERA, San Diego, CA, 1998.

Silbert, M. et al. (1980). *Sexual assault on prostitutes: Final report.* Washington, D.C.: National Institute of Mental Health, National Center for the Prevention and Control of Rape.

Silbert, M. & Pines, A. (1982). Entrance into prostitution. *Youth and Society, 13*(4), 471-500.

Simmons, R. (2002). *Odd girl out: The hidden culture of aggression in girls.* New York: Harcourt.

Sloan, L. & Wahab, S. (2000). Feminist voices on sex work: Implications for social work. *Affilia, 15*(4), 457-79.

Steedman, C. (1986). *Landscape for a good woman: A story of two lives.* London: Virago Press.

Steinem, G. (1992). *In the company of women: voices from the women's movement.* New York: Routledge.

Stephens, R. (1996). The art of safe schooling planning. *The School Administrator, 2* (53), 1.

Sullivan, M. L. (1989). *Getting paid.* Ithaca, NY: Cornell University Press.

Takacs, D. (2002). Positionality, epistemology and social justice in the classroom. *Social Justice, 29*(3), 168-81.

Tidwell, R. (1988). Dropouts speak out: qualitative data on early school departures. *Adolescence 23*(92), 939-954. San Diego: Libra Publishers.

Toronto Star. (2001). B.C. schools need more after three teens charged, parent says. March 29, p.NE07.

URSA. (1981). *An annotated bibliography on adolescent male and female prostitution and related topics.* San Francisco: Youth Development Bureau of the Dept. of Health and Human Services.

Vail, K. (2002). Relational aggression in girls. *The Education Digest, 68*(2), 7-14.

Walker, Alice. (1983). *In search of our mothers' gardens.* San Diego: Harcourt Brace Jovanovich.

Watkins, W. H. (2001). Blacks and the curriculum: From accommodation to contestation and beyond. In W. H. Watkins, J. H. Lewis, & V. Chou (Eds.), *Race and education: The roles of history and society in education African American students* (pp.40-60), Needham Heights, MA: Allyn & Bacon.

Wehmeyer, M. & Schwartz, M. (2001). Research on gender bias in special education services. In H. Rousso & M. Wehmeyer (Eds). *Double jeopardy: Addressing gender equity in special education* (pp. 271-288). Albany, NY: SUNY Press.

Wehlage, G.G. & Rutter, R. A. (1986). Dropping out: How much do schools contribute to the problem. *Teachers College Record, 87,* 374-392.

Weisberg, D. K. (1985). *Children of the night: A study of adolescent prostitution.* Lexington, MA: D.C. Heath.

Williams, T. (1989). *The cocaine kids.* New York: Addison-Wesley.

Williamson, C. (1999). *Entrance, maintenance, and exit: The socio-economic influences and cumulative burdens of female street prostitution.* Unpublished doctoral dissertation. Indiana Univeristy.

Wilson, J. (1994). Beauty rites: Towards an anatomy of culture in African American women's art. *The International Review of African American Art, 11*(3), 11-55.

Wilson, W. J. (1997). *When work disappears.* New York: Knopf.

Wiseman, R. (2003). *Queen bees and wannabes: Helping our daughters survive cliques, gossip, boyfriends, and other realities of adolescence.* New York: Three Rivers Press.

Women's Educational Equity Act Program (WEEAP). (1990). *Female dropouts: The challenge.* Washington, D.C.: Women's Educational Equity Act Publishing Center Digest.

Woodson, C.G. (1933). *The miseducation of the negro.* Washington, D.C.: Associated Publishers.

Wynter, S. (1987). WHISPER: Women hurt in systems of prostitution engaged in revolt. In F. Delacoste & P. Alexander (Eds.), *Sex work: Writings by women in the sex industry* (pp. 266-270). Pittsburgh, PA: Cleis.

Yates, L. (1993). *The education of girls: Policy, research and the question of gender.* Hawthorn, VIC: Austrialian Council for Educational Research.

Zatz, N. (1997). Sex work/sex act: Law labor, and desire in constructions of prostitution. *Signs, 22,* 277-308.

Studies in the Postmodern Theory of Education

General Editors
Joe L. Kincheloe & Shirley R. Steinberg

Counterpoints publishes the most compelling and imaginative books being written in education today. Grounded on the theoretical advances in criticalism, feminism, and postmodernism in the last two decades of the twentieth century, Counterpoints engages the meaning of these innovations in various forms of educational expression. Committed to the proposition that theoretical literature should be accessible to a variety of audiences, the series insists that its authors avoid esoteric and jargonistic languages that transform educational scholarship into an elite discourse for the initiated. Scholarly work matters only to the degree it affects consciousness and practice at multiple sites. Counterpoints' editorial policy is based on these principles and the ability of scholars to break new ground, to open new conversations, to go where educators have never gone before.

For additional information about this series or for the submission of manuscripts, please contact:

Joe L. Kincheloe & Shirley R. Steinberg
c/o Peter Lang Publishing, Inc.
29 Broadway, 18th floor
New York, New York 10006

To order other books in this series, please contact our Customer Service Department:

(800) 770-LANG (within the U.S.)
(212) 647-7706 (outside the U.S.)
(212) 647-7707 FAX

Or browse online by series:
www.peterlang.com